T0286920

True Crime Redux

STEPHANIE KANE

bancroft
press

Cover design by Christine Van Bree
Interior design by Marcel Venter and Tracy Copes

978-1-61088-611-6 HC
978-1-61088-610-9 PB
978-1-61088-609-3 Ebook
978-1-61088-607-9 Audio

Published by Bancroft Press
"Books that Enlighten"
(818) 275-3061
4527 Glenwood Avenue
La Crescenta, CA 91214
www.bancroftpress.com
Printed in the United States of America

In memory of Cherrie and Jean

Contents

Introduction

Persons Involved

Preface

1973

The Scene

Statements

Collateral Damage

The Right Man

The Right Woman

2005

The Cold Case

The Family

The Courtroom

Shooting the Survivors

Coda

About the Author

Introduction

Quiet Time, my first mystery, was a fictionalized version of the brutal murder of a suburban housewife. Not just any housewife, but Betty Frye, on the eve of my marriage to her son. Back in 1973, Doug and I were college students at CU in Boulder, practicing karate and living together on the Hill. The morning Betty was murdered, I spoke with her. Hours later, I saw her killer. Her death made me a crime writer.

Quiet Time was my lab for learning the craft of writing fiction. The manuscript underwent twenty-odd drafts, each more heavily fictionalized than the last. I wasn't imaginative enough to invent brand-new characters, though I did change the killer. And the ending was entirely made up, since in real life he'd walked. Having justice prevail made the story cathartic.

In 2001, when Bantam acquired *Quiet Time,* I was frank about its origins. I met with Bantam's legal team and made more changes. The book was published under a pen name to make its connection to Betty's murder even less recognizable, but the title itself escaped scrutiny: "quiet time" was what her kids called those times when Betty forbade them to make noise while she lay in the dark.

How much of *Quiet Time* was true?

Quiet Time's protagonist was a thinly-veiled version of me, a Jewish girl from Brooklyn who'd gone to CU to put 2,000 miles between her and her folks. Only, of course, to fall in love with a boy whose parents were bound to hate everything about her. Also true was the depiction of the day of Betty's murder: her phone call that morning to our apartment, and the unexpected arrival of her husband Duane at the karate studio, in clothes too heavy for the weather and bearing a nasty bruise on his head. Except Bantam made me change the karate studio to a hockey rink.

But *Quiet Time* wasn't based just on memories.

In 1973, Duane Frye had been indicted for his wife's murder. The charges were inexplicably dropped, and for the nine years during which I was married to their son, the crime was not discussed. After we divorced, I tunneled into an existence strangely like my protagonist's: corporate lawyer by day, haunted at night by Betty's murder and the feeling that somehow our wedding had been the catalyst for the explosion of rage that ended her life. By the early 1990s, it was time to put my ghosts to rest.

I'd remarried, and my new husband knew the District Attorney who'd prosecuted Duane in 1973. The DA told us the case was blown by an old-timer, a highway-patrol cop. He gave me some fragments of microfiche reports which mentioned a cop named Sendle, and a trip to the courthouse for the 1973 file yielded a white-on-gray transcript of Sendle's grand jury testimony. I couldn't tell how old Sendle was, but he seemed sharper than I'd expected. *Quiet Time*'s cop split the difference: paunchy Ray Burt, on the verge of retirement, haunted by his own ghosts, but with a certain savviness. For my catharsis, I needed someone who actually cared.

So, at Bantam's request, I moved *Quiet Time*'s timeline up ten years, changed Denver and Boulder to Widmark and

Stanley, and purged all references to karate and Colorado (though New Mexico was allowed to remain a neighboring state). When the novel came out, nobody connected it to Betty's murder. Published the week of 9/11, *Quiet Time* had a short life and a quick death.

Then in 2005, Duane's sister saw me interviewed on a late-night rerun of a canceled public TV show. She recognized me, read *Quiet Time,* and came forward with a murder confession her brother had made. A cold case was opened, and overnight my novel and I became targets of the defense. The theory was laughable: that I'd conspired with Duane's 78-year-old sister, whom I hadn't seen in thirty years, to fabricate his confession in order to sell books. Claiming each *Quiet Time* draft was a factual statement they could use to impeach me as a witness, Duane's lawyers subpoenaed all twenty-some of them, along with my correspondence and notes.

The subpoena placed my writing and thought process under direct attack. An excellent lawyer of my own, and the expert testimony of an English Lit professor, convinced the judge that although all fiction is based on fact, that doesn't *make* it fact. My drafts, etc. were eventually protected, but the subpoena made me question what I'd done to real people to exorcise my own ghosts. I'd published three legal thrillers since *Quiet Time,* but the threat of having my creative processes scrutinized paralyzed me. For the eight years the case was in court, I wrote not a word.

At the same time, in an Orwellian tit-for-tat, the defense's voluminous pleadings treated me to new versions of myself. Being described as the "former fiancée" of someone to whom you were married for almost a decade is darkly humorous, but not really funny. Nor is a courtroom the ideal place to face real people whom your fiction brought to life and caused to be re-indicted for murder. Witnesses are forbidden to contact each other, but that didn't stop one of my former sisters-in-law from brushing past me with a look of rage. I notice you're not coming to the family and saying, Would you like us to pursue this? she'd told the cold case cops. Nor did it stop Duane at the defense table screaming Liar! as I was on the witness stand.

But Betty's sisters embraced me. Octogenarians, they drove from as far as Kansas to show up for her in court, month after month. The day I testified, two tiny white-haired ladies were in the front row of the gallery, their faces turned trustingly to mine. Afterwards, the eldest whispered to me consolingly, We're not all like Betty. Because by then, everyone knew my wedding to Betty's son had indeed lit the match.

Persons Involved

Immediate Family

Elizabeth (Betty) Frye: 45-year-old housewife and murder victim

Herbert (Duane) Frye: Betty's 48-year-old husband

Jan Frye: 23-year-old daughter

Marilyn (Lynn) Frye: 21-year-old daughter

Doug Frye: 19-year-old son

Greg Frye: 13-year-old son

Relatives

Cora (Cundy) Orten: Betty's mother

Charley Orten: Betty's father

Jean Brickell: Betty's closest sister

Dick Brickell: Jean's husband

Lolita Frye: Duane's mother

Herbert (Inky) Frye: Duane's father

Cherrie Otto: Duane's sister

Hank Otto: Cherrie's former husband

Others

Barbara (Barb) Dean Frye: Duane's second wife

Jim Dean: Barbara's former husband

Investigators

Lieutenant Bob Sendle: Arapahoe County Sheriff's Office Chief of Investigations in 1973

Jim Blake: Duane's private detective in 1973

Bruce Isaacson: Arapahoe County Sheriff's Office lead cold case investigator in 2006

Marv Brandt: Isaacson's partner

Witnesses

Randy Peterson: Carpenter working on roof overlooking Frye backyard

Bret Wacker: Greg's best friend who came to Frye door

Virginia Moldenhauer: Betty's co-worker at Martin Marietta

Midge Krebs: Family friend who saw Duane, Betty, and Barb at The Holly Inn

Alternate Suspects

Tom Gussie: Small-time burglar

Bob Firth: Gussie's friend

Prosecutors

Bob Gallagher: Arapahoe County District Attorney in 1973

Jim DeRose and Jim Macrum: Arapahoe County Assistant District Attorneys in 1973

Ann Tomsic: Arapahoe County Chief Deputy District Attorney in 2006

Ryan Brackley: Arapahoe County Assistant District Attorney in 2008

Defense Lawyers

Leonard Davies: Duane's lead counsel in 1973

Gary Lozow: Duane's lead counsel in 2006

Hal Haddon: Stephanie's lawyer

Judges

Valeria Spencer: Arapahoe County District Judge in 2006

Charles Pratt: Arapahoe County District Judge in 2008

Preface

I. Just Start Telling the Story

It is the process of storytelling rather than the story itself that is the point. What excited Sarah Polley about making a documentary about her mother was watching the aftermath.
—**Sarah Polley | Filmmaker**

If there's a story you like, just write it up and see how it feels. It's not illegal until you do something with it.
—**Alan Sharp | Screenwriter**

My story begins on a hot Saturday morning in June 1973. The phone rang in the apartment I shared with my fiancé in Boulder, Colorado. I picked up because Doug was in the shower. It was his mother, Betty. She'd never called before, and this call was awkward and brief. Doug and I were getting married in two weeks and didn't know, even then, if she would be coming to the ceremony. Two hours later, she was dead.

I thought about that phone call for thirty years. Every night, I ran through my exchange with Betty and the events that followed. Sometimes it was the first thing on my mind when I woke up. I didn't want to forget. Even more than needing to understand her death, it was important to remember the details. In 2001, I published *Quiet Time,* a fictionalized version of Betty's murder. The nightmares stopped.

Then in 2005, I got an e-mail from a cold case cop looking into Betty's murder. He asked if I was willing to talk. I'd long since come to terms with not knowing the truth about that day but had never resolved my role in it. But this was bigger than me. The legal battle that followed consumed the next decade of my life.

Fifty years have passed since Betty's call. From a college-town apartment to a karate studio, from a blood-spattered suburban garage to a rogue ex-cop, law school, a mystery novel, grand jury indictments, subpoenas for a manuscript's drafts, trips up and down appellate courts, to a family irreparably fractured and turned on itself.

And at the heart of it all was a brutal murder.

2. Not From That Place

I don't have the advantage of being from there, from that region, of that race. But my responsibility is to tell stories, to tell the story I want to tell in the way I want to tell it. And if there are repercussions from that, I'll just have to face it.

—Bill Cheng | Author of *Southern Cross the Dog*

Locard's Exchange Principle: The theory that anyone, or anything, entering a crime scene both takes something of the scene with them, and leaves something of themselves behind when they leave.

—Brent Turvey | *Criminal Profiling: An Introduction to Behavioral Evidence Analysis*

I met Doug at a karate studio in Boulder, Colorado.

I'd applied to CU because it was 2,000 miles from Brooklyn. But the moment the plane landed, I was in over my head. The dry wind, blazing sky, and strapping kids playing frisbee on a campus backed by mountain peaks felt unreal, like a technicolor movie.

I wandered into a karate studio and watched my future husband, Doug, throwing one perfect kick after another.

With his crisp white gi and sun-streaked hair, he embodied everything foreign and exotic about Colorado. We moved in together that summer. And that fall he brought me home to meet his parents.

Home was a tract house in a suburb south of Denver. Doug's father, Duane, was an engineer whose kids called him "Mr. Work the Problem." His mother, Betty, was a stylish blonde straight out of *Vogue* or *Better Homes & Gardens*. Doug told her I was a vegetarian majoring in Italian, so she served melon and provolone.

Duane was *Field & Stream*. Over dinner, he railed against Texans snatching up prime Colorado mountain property, and an East Coast cabal that he believed controlled the news media.

I might have debated Duane, but I was too intimidated and intent on being liked. The following June, on the morning Betty was murdered, Duane showed up at the karate studio unannounced, with a bruise on his forehead and a warm six-pack of beer.

Doug's family was foreign but enticingly normal—or at least how I fantasized a normal family would be. But it's impossible to know any family's truth. And being an outsider makes that truth even harder to see. In telling their story the way I wanted to tell it, *Quiet Time* initiated a cold case but barely scratched the truth.

Families are also like crime scenes. Entering one, you bring something with you. Leaving, you bear its mark. The very act changes that family's story and makes you of that place. The story continues to be reshaped by the marks you leave on each other each time you collide.

3. Memory and Procrustean Narratives

memory/1 The faculty by which things are remembered; the capacity for retaining, perpetuating, or reviving the thought of things past.
—*The New Shorter Oxford Dictionary*

Procrustean/ Of or pertaining to Procrustes, a robber who in Greek legend stretched or mutilated his victims in order to make them fit the length of his bed.
—*The New Shorter Oxford Dictionary*

Frequently, our only truth is narrative truth, the stories we tell each other, and ourselves—the stories we continually recategorize and refine. Such subjectivity is built into the very nature of memory, and follows from its basis and mechanisms in the human brain. The wonder is that aberrations of a gross sort are relatively rare, and that, for the most part, our memories are solid and reliable.
—**Oliver Sacks** | *Speak, Memory*

This is what I remember about Saturday, June 9, 1973:

I remember Betty's call that morning. The hopeful look on Doug's face that said, maybe she's coming around. Doug's 13-year-old brother, Greg, coming for his first karate lesson. Me sneaking into the empty pool next door because it was already so hot. Seeing Duane on the studio bench in a white T-shirt under a dark, long-sleeved plaid shirt. The bruise on his forehead. A lawn chair fell while he was doing spring cleanup with Betty, he said. She hadn't told me he was coming. Why was Duane there? To pick up Greg, he said, and to show him your apartment.

The last time we saw Betty was at the Flagstaff House, a fancy restaurant above Boulder where they'd taken us to celebrate our engagement. When Duane toasted our future, she cried, and when they dropped us off, she wouldn't come in. She made us promise her one thing: that Greg would never know we'd lived together before getting married.

After the karate class, Duane drove us home to the apartment. He gave Doug a six-pack—not 3.2 beer but the real stuff, warm from the car. While Greg looked around, Duane sat on our daybed with his head in his hands. Then he abruptly stood and said they had to go. I wonder what's wrong, Doug said. I've never seen him act like this.

We left to pick up Doug's wedding suit—his first suit ever. When we got back, the phone was ringing. Come home, a neighbor said. Your mother's dead.

In 1973, the only person who interviewed me was Duane's defense investigator. He liked my description of Duane's clothes. No one asked about Betty's call, the beer, or the bruise.

When you don't know the bigger story, all you have are the details. From them, you weave a hopeful narrative: She called because she was coming around. He gave Doug the beer because he recognized his son was a man. All will be okay if Greg never knows. But what about the bruise?

Because details don't fit a story that's wrong, it doesn't mean you got the details wrong. Years later, defense lawyers will pound you in briefs and on the stand. You're out on a limb, no one else saw it. After so long, how can you be sure? But the stubbornness of those memories—the fact that they don't fit— makes them indelible. And you retained them because you re-categorized your narrative into a new one of hope: That one day you would know.

4. Casting Roles

role/1 An actor's part in a play, film, etc.; the part played or assumed by a person in society, life, etc.

---

scapegoat/1 In the biblical ritual of the Day of Atonement (Lev.16), a goat chosen by lot to be sent into the wilderness, after the chief priest had symbolically laid the sins of the people on it (while another goat was appointed to be sacrificed). **2** A person or thing blamed or punished for a mistake, fault, etc. of another or others.
—*The New Shorter Oxford English Dictionary*

The suffering Duane Frye has been caused is a real tragedy, defense lawyer Leonard Davies said. He noted again, as he had in a preliminary hearing, that the sheriff's department, in his opinion, had refused to pursue an eye witness, and that the case [against Duane] was dismissed because it was totally improper.

Lt. Robert Sendle of the department noted in the hearing that while he did not personally check out a report of a witness (a construction worker at a home in sight of the Frye home), he assigned a co-worker to do so. Apparently, the check was made some time after the information was given. Frye claimed he found his wife lying on the ground at 5:30 p.m. after returning from Boulder, where he was trying to arrange a wedding reception for his son, who was soon to be married.

The grand jury indictment, according to Davies, was based solely on testimony from Sendle. After Frye was indicted, the grand jury interviewed neighbors and acquaintances of the Fryes. Only one person—a child—had placed Frye at the murder scene around the time of the killing, Davies said.

—*Littleton Independent*, **November 29, 1973**

When I remarried in 1993, I told my new husband, John, about Betty's murder. He wanted to know why the charges against Duane had been dropped. John is a judge. Loose ends and the evasion of justice offend him. He'd also gone to law school with Bob Gallagher, who had prosecuted the case back in 1973. Gallagher agreed to meet with us.

Gallagher was avuncular and twinkly-eyed, but his memory of the housewife killed in her garage in Littleton was hazy. The case was blown by an old-timer, he said—a guy from the Colorado State Patrol. They didn't investigate cases then the way they do now. Gallagher sent me a handful of microfiche reports, mostly fragments, barely legible.

I went to the Littleton courthouse for the case file. Attached to a 1973 defense motion was the grand jury transcript of one Robert D. a/k/a Bob a/k/a Bobby Dale Sendle. Was he the old-timer Gallagher described? I pictured Sendle as a cross between Broderick Crawford and Barney Fife. In the transcript, Sendle laid out the case, and he was anything but stupid. Leonard Davies, Duane's defense attorney, had to take him down.

Every story needs a villain and a hero. In a crime, the cast expands to three: the perp, the victim, and the cop. Like a new director coming on set, Davies recast these roles. He made Duane the victim, Sendle the fall guy, and Betty a bit player in the drama of her own murder. Those roles were so successful they were reprised forty years later in the cold case. And I, too, used Sendle.

Sendle's 1973 transcript became a basis for *Quiet Time,* my 2001 mystery novel about Betty's murder. But, in real life, her killer had walked. My story had to end differently. So I reinvented Sendle as Ray Burt, a well-intentioned bumbler of a cop on the verge of retirement, because I needed to believe somebody cared.

In 2014, I met with Sendle at an RV resort southeast of Phoenix where he and his wife spent their winters. Sendle was different than I'd imagined: tall, keen-eyed, blunt. He walked me through the crime; unlike Gallagher, he remembered every detail. In 2005, when Duane was interviewed by cold case detectives, he fixated on a cop he claimed had tried to kill him on the stand back then. Now I understood why. No recasting or reinvention could change Bob Sendle.

5. You're Not That Important

In 1961, Leonid Rogozov, a young surgeon at the Soviet research station in Antarctica, had appendicitis. Winter was setting in, there were no flights out, and the ship that brought him wouldn't return for a year. He wrote in his diary, "Still no obvious symptoms that perforation is imminent, but an oppressive feeling of foreboding hangs over me. I have to think through the only possible way out—to operate on myself.... It's almost impossible... but I can't just fold my arms and give up." With a local anesthetic and working by touch, he cut into his abdominal wall. "Well, I thought, it's going to end badly and all that was left was removing the appendix." Rogozov survived his auto-appendectomy and was back at work in two weeks. He returned to Russia hating Antarctica but as a national hero.
—**Sara Lentati | BBC World**

I'm no hero in any story, not mine or Betty's.

In February 1973, four months before she was murdered, I learned I was pregnant. *Roe vs. Wade* had just become law. The decision to have an abortion made the future serious, and Doug and I decided to marry at the end of the school year. Right before Mother's Day, without telling me, he told his parents about the abortion. Betty cried. Did my abortion light a match?

The night of the murder, after Doug and I were summoned to their Littleton home, I walked to a nearby pay phone to call my mom. A couple of days later, she flew to Colorado. She already knew about the abortion, and now I told her about Duane's bruise, his heavy clothing on a hot summer day, his weird behavior at our apartment. She cut me off. You don't really know anything, do you? she said. And think what it'd do to Doug.

But Mom, I said, I think Betty died because of me, because of something I did.

You're not that important, Mom replied.

The cops didn't interview me in 1973, and I didn't speak to them. Was telling my mother enough? She was probably trying to protect me, but why did I buy into her line? It was easier to believe I knew nothing, that stealing Betty's son and aborting Betty's first grandchild were non-events.

More than anything, I hoped Mom was right. In 2008, when Duane's lawyers pummeled me on the stand on what they called my duty to come forward, it was nothing compared to the nightly auto-appendectomies I'd undergone for thirty-five years. And by Year 35, I knew the truth.

In 2005, the cold case cop who contacted me had two

questions: Did I know where the murder weapon was, and did I have an abortion in 1973?

Somewhere between Leonid Rogozov and total insignificance, I fit into the story. Because it wasn't just Betty's story. It was also mine.

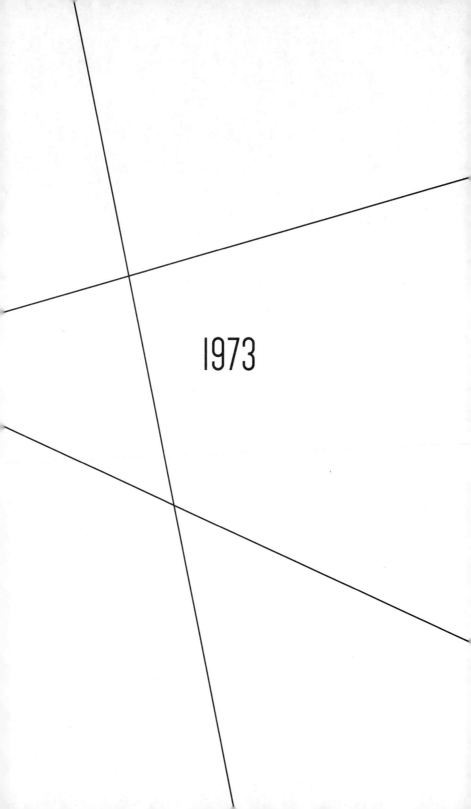

1973

6. Story Worlds

Stories must obey their own internal laws of probability.
—**Robert McKee | *Story: Substance, Structure, Style, and the Principles of Screenwriting***

What was taken? Was anything taken? I don't recall anything being taken. I said, doesn't that seem a little weird and a, a fluke? You know, a relatively affluent, white-collar neighborhood that somebody would, in the middle of a beautiful day, just kill somebody for no reason? Well, you know, so what are you implying? I said, Well, I'm not implying anything. It just doesn't make any sense to me.
—**Don Beckett | 2008**

Visualize a brick-and-clapboard house with a carriage lamp over the mailbox, just off the busy thoroughfare of Arapahoe Road. Pan to a cop ticketing a motorcycle and a VW bug on Arapahoe. Across the road and cater-corner to the house, three carpenters are installing siding on a new home. Zoom out over a tidy subdivision of suburban tract homes where residents are watering lawns, feeding roses, and hanging clothes on a brilliant Saturday morning in June 1973.

Because the houses have been platted to face the street, each backyard abuts the yard of the neighbor behind it. Directly behind this house is where the Hardings live. Doug was buddies with their son; he knew him in high school and roomed with him their freshman year at CU. Rosa Lee Harding was the only neighbor who saw anything unusual the day Betty was murdered.

At 10:00 a.m., Mrs. Harding watered the flowers in her backyard. She hung out her first load of laundry between 10:15 and 10:30, and the second at 11:30. Between the first and second loads, she heard a noise from Betty's house, like something fell. The time would prove crucial after a neighbor boy said he'd been to the Frye house that morning looking for Doug's kid brother Greg, and Duane answered the door.

Places are more than locations. They form a sticky web. A house backs onto its neighbor's and a woman hears a noise. A carpenter sees a cop giving tickets and a man in a yard. A kid goes looking for his friend and finds someone else. Thirty-five years later, Doug's sister's boyfriend remembers that nothing fit. When a world defies its internal laws of probability, people notice.

7. False Narratives

One of the most common instances in which crime scene staging is encountered is in a domestic homicide where a spouse is murdered at the family residence. In these cases, perpetrators are aware that if the spouse's body is discovered at the unaltered scene, they will immediately become the primary suspect.
—**Richard Walton** | *Cold Case Homicides: Practical Investigative Techniques*

When a scene is staged, the game has been set in motion. It pits the offender against a society represented by the investigator.
—**Richard Kocsis and George Palermo** | *Offender Profiling: An Introduction to the Sociopsychological Analysis of Violent Crime*

No mortal can keep a secret. If his lips are silent, he chatters with his fingertips; betrayal oozes out of him at every pore.
—**Sigmund Freud**

Every crime scene tells a story. A staged one tells conflicting narratives, one of which is false. The perp plays a cat-and-mouse game. Because he can't keep a secret or because his behavioral traits are fixed, he leaves thought-prints. An amateur with no idea what a real crime scene looks like makes mistakes. Under pressure to act fast, he makes more mistakes. If he's gamey to begin with, he overthinks and overworks the problem.

Betty was killed in what looked like a burglary gone bad. Her house was in disarray, and she was found face-down on the garage floor. Near the garage's overhead door were a couple of TVs and two garbage cans which had been taken from the utility room to cart away stolen loot. The garbage cans held a wrapped gift, kitchen items, an electric shaver, an open bottle of shampoo, a pair of clip-on Ray-Bans, and three electric clocks. The killer was careful: He used gloves and wiped everything clean.

But he blew it with the clocks. When they were unplugged from the wall, they stopped: the master bedroom's at 11:22, the kitchen's at 11:23, and Greg's clock-radio at 11:27. The clocks didn't just shadow Betty's killer through the house. They also showed when she was killed. In order to deposit the house loot in the garbage cans, her murderer had to track through her blood.

Burglars are different from killers. Furtive and conflict-avoidant, they target residences during the week and businesses on weekends. Before breaking into a house, they make sure nobody's home. If confronted, they run. Betty's murder occurred just off a busy intersection in a bustling subdivision on a beautiful Saturday morning in June. Her front door was unlocked, but the killer apparently entered and left by a street-side gate that had always been wired shut from the inside.

A staged crime scene physically manifests a lie. Like a dummy's ventriloquist, the crime scene's true voice is the perp's. But cops are trained skeptics, not human lie detectors. DAs and defense lawyers each have a dog in the fight. Courts are concerned with a larger truth: justice. The telling and accepting of lies—letting ourselves be deceived—rests with us. He couldn't have done it. He's not the type. How could a smart guy like him make such stupid mistakes?

Crime has no secrets. Eventually, the game is up.

8. Show, Don't Tell

Show, don't tell is a technique to allow the reader to experience the story through action, words, thoughts, senses, and feelings rather than through the author's exposition, summarization, and description. It describes the scene in such a way that the reader can draw his or her own conclusions.
—*Wikipedia*

---

snapshot/2: an impression or view of something brief or transitory.
—*Merriam-Webster's Collegiate Dictionary, Eleventh Edition*

Like a photographer framing a shot, a writer selects details that show more than they tell. Crime scenes are different. What is telling is in the eye of the beholder.

Going through a trash can filled with stolen loot in the Frye garage in 1973, Bob Sendle was struck by a pair of Ray Bans. Why would a burglar steal clip-on sunglasses? When he interviewed Duane, he noticed that Duane wore glasses. You wear sunglasses? Sendle asked. Yes, Duane said, clip-ons. He reached in his shirt pocket, but to his surprise, they weren't there. Sendle never forgot the look on Duane's face. Course he didn't have them, Sendle told me many years later. He dropped them when he was leaning over that trash barrel filling it with loot.

Forty years after Betty was murdered, when I saw the crime-scene photographs for the first time, something else jumped out. At the top of one of the cans was a rectangular package, wrapped in silver paper with cupids and doves. It had a shiny ribbon and a stick-on bow. I pictured Duane running through the house after he killed Betty, grabbing things that made no sense to a burglar and meant nothing to him. Not Duane's expensive shotguns. Not stuff a burglar could fence, but cheap clocks and appliances, a TV with a broken antenna, and a wedding gift.

In a photo taken at our wedding later that summer, Doug and I rejoice. My new father-in-law grins as he pours us champagne. Moments earlier, he'd handed us a wrapped gift. Eagerly, I'd torn off the cupid-and-doves paper and shiny bow. Inside were two long-stemmed, silver-plated wine glasses. From Betty and me, Duane said as he toasted us with glasses he'd thrown in the trash moments after beating his wife to death.

Without even knowing their history, Doug and I never drank from those wine glasses again. When Doug left nine years later, he didn't take them with him. When I remarried, I gave them to Goodwill.

9. Cut!

bystander: one present but not taking part in a situation or event: a chance spectator.

---

edit/1 c: to alter, adapt, or refine, esp. to bring about conformity to a standard or to suit a particular purpose; **3:** DELETE

---

cutting room: a room where film or videotape is edited—often used attributively in *cutting-room floor* to describe something removed or discarded in or as if in editing a film.
—Merriam-Webster's Collegiate Dictionary, Eleventh Edition

Innocent bystanders are a staple of stand-up comedians and cartoonists. Who can't relate to an ordinary Joe who happens onto something grisly or grotesque? But a bystander who stumbles onto a crime scene is no joke He's a defense lawyer's worst nightmare because he has no stake in the case. Duane's bogeyman was thirteen-year-old Bret Wacker.

Bret was Greg Frye's best friend. He lived one block from Greg, a three- minute walk. The morning Betty was killed, Bret wanted Greg to go with him to the 7-Eleven. He rang the Frye doorbell twice and then Duane answered.

Bret insisted this happened shortly after 11:30 a.m. The clocks with the loot in the garage near Betty's body stopped at 11:22, 11:23 and 11:27. If Bret was right, Duane's house was being burglarized while Duane was answering his own front door.

Timing was why Bret came forward. When a neighborhood kid told the Wackers he heard Betty was murdered between 10:00 a.m. and 5:00 p.m., Bret said it couldn't have been before 11:30 because he was at the Frye house. He was certain of the time because he'd been watching *The Monkees* and switched the channel to *Sherlock Holmes* for his brother just before he left the house.

Bret told his mother he'd be home in an hour, and she looked at the clock and thought, he better be back by 12:30. The *T.V. Guide* for June 9, 1973 said *The Monkees* ran from 11:00 a.m. to 11:30 on Channel 9 and *Sherlock Holmes* began at 11:30 on Channel 2.

Duane's defense team had three ways to deal with Bret: change his time of arrival, alter his testimony to favor Duane, or discredit him as a child. Duane's alibi for the crucial hour and a half that morning was jam-packed with trips to a Safeway, a liquor store, and a mega-mall, and two visits to a nearby Chevron station where he'd left Betty's car.

Confronted by the cops, Duane first admitted Bret came over looking for Greg, but claimed it was an hour earlier. The *T.V. Guide* nixed that. Employing Plan A, Duane's defense investigator, Jim Blake, monkied with the timeline. He put Bret's arrival at between 11:45 a.m. and 11:57.

To account for Duane's presence at the house when Bret arrived, Blake made Duane's morning still more chaotic. He added a third visit by Duane to the Chevron to retrieve a jacket he claimed he'd left in Betty's car. Duane then supposedly returned home just long enough to throw his jacket in the front hall closet a minute or two before Bret rang the bell.

Employing Plan B, Blake, in his report to Duane's lawyers, wrote that Bret said Duane was dirty because he'd been doing something with a car seat. This was a whopper. In 1973, Bret's father refused to let Blake interview his son, and Bret told both the cops and the grand jury Duane had no dirt or stains on his clothes. Was Blake trying to explain away the bruise on Duane's forehead? Finally, defense lawyer Leonard Davies jumped in with Plan C. He told the *Littleton Independent* the only person who placed Duane at the scene of the killing at the time it took place was a child.

Forty years later, Bret Wacker was a tech company executive. He remembered going to his best friend's house the day Greg's mother was killed. He remembered Duane answering the door. As a boy, he'd walked into a murder scene. As a man, he knew he was lucky to be alive. The cold case dragged on for years. Duane's lawyers called dozens of witnesses, but never Bret. They left him on the cutting-room floor.

10. Stock Characters

A stock character is a stereotypical fictional character in a novel, play, film, or a movie whom audiences recognize from frequent recurrences in a particular literary tradition. The point of the stock character is to move the story along by allowing the audience to already understand the character.
—*Wikipedia*

The characters in commedia dell'arte usually represent fixed social types and stock characters, such as foolish old men, devious servants, or military officers full of false bravado.
—*Wikipedia*

In a 1973 crime scene photograph, a cop in the Frye backyard peers at the lower crossbar of a six-foot fence. Past the fence, cater-corner to the yard, looms a house under construction. Its scaffolding is the perfect vantage point for observing the Frye yard. If the cop in the photo had looked up instead of down, he would have seen the scaffolding. He would have found the carpenters installing siding 65 yards away and asked what they saw. Duane's investigator Jim Blake did. The day of the murder, one of those carpenters, Randy Peterson, saw Betty and her killer.

About 10:00 that morning, Randy saw a petite woman, late thirties or maybe forty, with light brown hair like the color of the brick on the house, exit the back door to shake out a mop or rug. He watched her for ten or fifteen seconds. About then, he lost a contact lens. All three carpenters got on the ground and scrambled around looking for it. When Randy went to his car for his glasses, his dashboard clock said 10:10 or 10:12 a.m.

An hour later, Randy saw a man come out of the back door of the Frye garage. This occurred ten or twenty minutes before the DJ on Randy's radio said it was 11:30 a.m. Randy saw the man only in profile. The man was five-nine or ten and had dark hair cut to the middle of his ear. He wore jeans and an untucked dress shirt and walked past the dog-run toward the sidegate with a bounce. Not a tired-out step, Randy said, but kind of youthful. Not casual—sprightly. Based on his hair, gait, clothing, and profile, Randy thought the man was 16 to 19 years old. In 1973, Duane was five-nine and 150 pounds, with light brown hair. He was 48 years old.

The carpenters also saw a pickup truck parked in front of the Frye house. Randy thought it was gray; the others said green. The sunglasses Randy wore over his contacts accounted for the difference and why he described Betty's hair and the house's brick as light brown instead of blond. They would also darken the man's hair two or three shades.

But what made him youthful was his gait. Thirty-five years later, cold case cop Bruce Isaacson had an answer for that. If I'd just beaten my wife to death with a golf club, he said, I might walk with a bounce too.

The Scene

II. Description

description/1a: discourse intended to give a mental image of something experienced.
—*Merriam-Webster's Collegiate Dictionary, Eleventh Edition*

I helped my wife clean up the mess in the garage. The blood was up on the wall at least six or seven feet. My wife used a broom to get it washed off the wall. The body was lying with the feet near [a car stop ledge], and the head right near the leg of the saw-table. As I moved the saw-table to clean, blood kept flowing out from under the table. This happened each time I moved the table. We eventually got the mess cleaned up. The flies were starting to gather, and the blood was getting smelly. I didn't know Duane very well, we built a fence together, this one (pointing), and he and I got along well together.
—Ross Hobby | 1973

When we arrived at the Frye house with Doug's sisters Lynn and Jan late that afternoon, the ambulance was in the driveway. The cop out front said move on, can't you see there's been a tragedy here? Lynn's boyfriend told him we were family and he waved us to the curb.

The house teemed with cops, and Betty's kitchen counters were sooty from fingerprint powder. Duane took us on a tour of the ransacked bedrooms upstairs. Then he sat us at the dining room table. After he and Greg found Betty's body, he said, he'd sent Greg to the Hobbys next door for help. Stay out of the garage, he warned us. The case file says why.

The ambulance beat the deputy coroner to the scene. The deputy coroner stopped the crew from rolling Betty's body over and tracking through the blood on the garage floor. Spatter had traveled fifteen feet to the ceiling. An Air Force vet, the deputy coroner thought Betty had been shot in the head with a large caliber rifle or a shotgun. As the sun set, cops crawled the backyard looking for shotgun wadding. Doug and I got on our knees and helped them search.

The next morning, Betty was autopsied. The autopsy report said her mock turtleneck blouse was soaked with blood. The front of her shorts, her upper thighs, and her bare feet were covered with dirt from the garage floor. Her arms and face were crusted with blood, and a large amount of it clung to her shoulder-length blond hair. Her head had two deep wounds, one a semi-circle and the other star-shaped. Bone was driven into her brain. Both eyes were blackened. She was bludgeoned, choked on her own blood, and bled to death.

After Betty's body was washed, it was photographed. She looked more like a teenage girl than a 45-year-old mother of four. When I saw the photos of her on that metal table decades later, only then did the weight of her death truly hit.

12. Clues

In 2008, sixty-year-old Clue was given a makeover. "A board game is basically a story that you're telling around the table together," the designer said. "In this case, it's a murder mystery." To appeal to a new generation, Colonel Mustard was recast as a former football star and Victor Plum as a video game designer. The weapons were updated too: the lead pipe was scrapped, the revolver became a Colt M1911 pistol, and a trophy, an axe, and a baseball bat made their débuts.
—NPR | August 2008

In 2005, the cold case cops asked me what the murder weapon had been. Because Duane had been so possessive of the standing red tool chest in his garage, in *Quiet Time* I'd made the weapon a long-handled steel hammer with a milled face and a rip claw. But I had no clue.

Betty suffered massive injuries to her head. The scene was so bloody the cops first thought she'd been shot with a shotgun while she was face down on the garage floor. Near her body, they found a blood-soaked piece of plywood, and at the autopsy a splinter in her hair. But wood even twice that thick could not drive bone into her brain. The weapon had to be fairly sharp, like a small hatchet. Bob Sendle kept to himself his theory about the murder weapon. In 2014, he told me it was a golf club.

It's easy to clean, Sendle said, and a nine iron was missing from the golf bag in the garage. He expanded on his theory. You get mad at your wife and you're steaming. You cold-cock her and then realize what you've done and it's too late. You hit her fifteen times and maybe you meant to hit her once. If she's down and you're doing it fast, you'd use short blows to make sure she didn't get up, because you're scared if she does, you won't get another chance. That explained Duane's bruise: the club rebounded and hit him in his forehead.

The cold case cops agreed. By 2006, Duane had moved to a gated, deed-restricted community in Florida. His new house backed onto a golf course.

You golf? Bruce Isaacson asked him. I never touched a club, Duane said. Except just that once, Isaacson thought.

In 2007, a crime scene analyst revisited the Frye garage. New owners had painted the walls and drywalled the rafters. But the analyst was sharp. He pinpointed the location of the blood in the crime scene photos. Back at his lab, he tried to replicate the spatter with a Styrofoam mock-up of Betty's head, a wig similar to her hair, and a sponge soaked with horse blood.

Varying the angle of the blows, he struck the dummy's head multiple times with three different weapons: a baseball bat, the flat hammer side of an axe, and a nine iron with an aluminum shaft. Overhead swings with the golf club produced spatter closest to that found in 1973.

The analyst also identified a stain on the back of Betty's blouse. The killer had wiped a bloody object on it as she lay dying on the garage floor.

13. Props

prop 2: something used in creating or enhancing a desired effect.
—Merriam-Webster's Collegiate Dictionary

---

wooden gate open on right side of house open – hadn't been opened for years
gate was flapping – concerned
went into house – Greg – a few feet behind or in front
—Duane Frye | Arapahoe County Sheriff's Office Notes, June 1973

---

got home pulled in driveway – gate open
dad noticed gate first – never left open
went in with father –
—Greg Frye | Arapahoe County Sheriff's Office Notes, June 1973

It's not unusual to stage a domestic homicide as a burglary-gone-wrong. What's intriguing is how some of these killers use gates. In *Cold Case Homicides: Practical Investigative Techniques*, LA homicide detective Richard H. Walton recounts a brutal daytime murder in an upscale neighborhood. There was no forced entry or reports of screams, dogs barking, or strangers in the area. But days earlier, the husband had removed vegetation from the back gate to make it operational. Because he also left the front door wide open, directing attention to the gate suggests another characteristic common in staged domestic homicides: overkill.

Betty's murderer used a gate too.

The Frye house and garage were just feet from the curb. The backyard was surrounded by a six-foot wooden fence with a gate opening onto the street next to the garage. The gate was wired shut from the inside with a clothes hanger twisted around a post bolted to the garage. The gate was hard to see from the street because it was made from the same slats as the fence. With no trees or shrubs to provide cover from the street, fumbling with the gate to gain access to the backyard would have increased a burglar's risk of being seen. The Fryes didn't lock their doors. The only logical way in and out of the house was the unlocked front door.

Greg told the cops that when he and his father arrived home the day of the murder, Duane remarked that the gate was open. The wooden gate is open, he said. I wonder why it is open. It has never been open before. Cops found the hanger securing it untwisted and pieces of wire on the ground. But there is more to this gate's story.

Around 11:30 a.m., when Greg's friend Bret rang the

doorbell and Duane answered, the gate was closed. (Bret told the cops he would've noticed if it was open because it was never open before.) Ten or twenty minutes earlier, Randy Peterson, the carpenter installing siding at the home cater-corner to the Fryes, saw a man exit the back of the Frye house, cross the yard, and fiddle with the gate from the inside. The man was in no hurry and didn't look around to see if he was being watched. The clocks with the loot in the garage had been unplugged from the wall right about the time Bret was there and Peterson saw the intruder.

It's understandable why Duane would draw attention to his gate. But unless the man Peterson saw fiddling with the gate was Duane, Duane was home while his wife's killer was roaming his backyard and looting his house.

14. Setups

Setups are planted to have one meaning at first, but with a rush of insight take on a new and deeper meaning later.
—**Robert McKee** | *Story: Substance, Structure, Style, and the Principles of Screenwriting*

---

ambush/1: a trap in which concealed persons lie in wait to attack by surprise
—*Merriam-Webster's Collegiate Dictionary, Eleventh Edition*

The Frye house had a utility room with a walk-through door to the garage. Betty was found on the garage floor just past that door. She'd been attacked from behind, and there were no defensive wounds or signs of a struggle. In 1973, Duane told the cops that Saturday morning they'd been getting ready for summer, including cleaning out the garage. He cleaned the windows and mirrors in the upstairs bathroom and went to the store for more window cleaner because the plastic bottle was broken. I came home and finished up the job, Duane said.

The garage was small and cluttered. Near Betty's body were a couple of TVs and two garbage cans containing cheap appliances, the electric clocks, and a half-empty bottle of shampoo. Duane's gun cabinet was untouched, but the rest of the house was in disarray. Drawers were pulled part-way out of the master bedroom bureau, and Greg's night stand was tipped over. Sheets were bunched and stripped from beds, as if Betty had been interrupted while doing the weekend wash.

Blood spatter in a crime scene photograph shows the killer struck the right side of her head from high up and kept swinging once she was down. But another photo adds a more chilling detail.

In it, Betty lies face down on the dirt-covered cement floor. She wears shorts and a sleeveless mock-turtleneck blouse. She is barefoot. Three feet behind her, the walk-through door is half open. A four-step ladder stands to the door's right—the side that opens into the garage and is directly behind where Betty's body lies. The ladder is open. Instead of surprising a burglar, Bob Sendle thought Betty had been hit by someone who was standing on the ladder when she stepped through the door. Cold case prosecutor Ann Tomsic took it a step further. She believed the killer didn't just lie in wait. He had summoned Betty to the garage.

Something else can be discerned from that photograph. Betty took pride in her home and her appearance. What woman steps barefoot into a garage with a dirt- covered floor while she's in the middle of cleaning house? Only if she's called there by someone determined to finish his job.

15. Conflict

That man was out to kill me.
—Duane Frye, 2006

Conflict starts before antagonists meet. It is rooted in character and shaped by upbringing, fortune, and pursuits. Character is destiny. By the time conflict bursts full-fledged onto page or screen, the outcome is ordained. At the crime scene in 1973, Bob Sendle knew Betty's killer was no burglar before he even met the man.

In the Frye master bedroom, two drawers stood upright on the floor. That was strange: burglars dumped drawers out to rifle through their contents quickly. The ones in the dresser were pulled out the same distance. That, too, was odd: to look inside, a burglar would've had to pull each drawer farther out or push the previous ones back in. The game was on. But it had begun decades earlier, in Depression era Kansas and east-central Oklahoma.

Bob Sendle was born and raised by a single mother in Oklahoma. The only time he and his big brother heard from their dad was at Christmas, when they'd get a piece of candy or maybe a pair of Levis. When Bob was nine, their mom died and maternal aunts took them in. But he and his brother were country boys, throwing rocks and breaking church windows, and they wound up in an orphanage.

One night, they snuck out to a movie. The next day, the superintendent summoned their dad to pick them up. He took them to a filthy trailer in Clarendon, Texas. There was a fight, and the boys pooled their money for a bus out of town. Sixty years later, Bob Sendle could draw a map of every room in that orphanage but he couldn't say he ever really knew his father.

Sendle dropped out of high school to join the Marines because his brother told him he'd never make it through boot camp. He got his values from his brother, boxing, and the Marine Corps, and being thrown out of an orphanage and forced to live with a father he'd never laid eyes on in the middle of nowhere.

In 2014, I met Sendle and Ginny, his wife of 51 years, and their toy poodles Elvis and Rocky. By then, Bob had retired as chief of police in a town in Minnesota. Though barely thirty years old in 1973, he wasn't intimidated by a suspect who was twenty years older.

Duane grew up in Atwood, Kansas, the Rawlins County seat. His father, a depressed and gentle man, owned Frye Auto & Electric. His mother had a gift shop in town and despised "Bohunks," the Czech farmers living in the valley.

During World War II, Duane enrolled in the V-12 Naval College Training program but flunked out of midshipmen's school because he was too busy partying. After the war, he got an engineering degree from CU and worked at Honeywell and Stanley Aviation. He believed fervently in Ayn Rand, the libertarian philosopher and author for whom the individual existed solely for his own sake. Duane was an avid hunter. His dogs were working animals, not pets. He kept them in a run behind his garage.

Shortly before Betty was killed, Duane was laid off by Martin Marietta. At the Arapahoe County Sheriff's Office with his lawyer days after his wife's murder, he handed Sendle two business cards. One identified him as Executive VP and Treasurer at a land development company called Leisure Villas. The other said he was Director of Corporate Development at an outfit called Data Corp. Both companies had the same address and phone number.

Bob Sendle was Duane Frye's worst nightmare because Duane prided himself on the very things for which Sendle had no use. From their first encounter, Sendle was in Duane's head. And he never left.

Statements

16. Point of View

Point of view: the perspective from which a scene is written, which character's eyes and minds are witnessing the event.
—**Sol Stein** | *Stein on Writing*

This is a very disturbed individual. He is a child whose emotional disposition is far beyond his physical age. He would not think like a child of [thirteen] and would resent being treated like one. This person has a morbid curiosity and he would be capable of erotic, irrational acts. This child needs help and he is headed for trouble, if not already in trouble.
—**Handwriting Analysis of Gregory Frye | Andrew J. Bradley, Document Examiner, Arapahoe County Sheriff's Office, 1973**

Maybe [Greg] was eating, he was down in the living room, but he wasn't showing the emotion I expected of him either. He was sitting in the living room eating something. There was something awkward about it, it didn't make sense.
—**Bob Sendle | 2014**

The Greg I knew was a skinny kid with sandy hair, sloping shoulders, and a shy grin. The morning his mother was killed, he'd come to Boulder to take his first karate class from his big brother Doug. When Doug and I arrived at the Frye house in Littleton late that afternoon, Greg was standing on the lawn crying. Greg gave the cops a written statement. In eight lines of neat cursive, with no corrections or cross-outs, he recounted his day and referred to Betty as "her."

Greg's statement started with rising at 9:15 a.m. and having breakfast, and ended with returning home from Boulder and seeing the gate open and upstairs drawers disturbed. At the Sheriff's Office three days later, he told investigators his dad sent him upstairs to check out his room before telling him to go get the neighbors.

After the funeral, Duane put Greg on a plane to Betty's sister Lucene in California. Lu's kids behaved. Greg was so out of control Lu thought he was on drugs. Greg finally told Lu he saw his mom's body on the garage floor. Years later, he thanked Lu for saving his life.

The Greg I knew had a piggybank and hid candy under his bed. Did good penmanship spell trouble to document examiner Bradley, as Greg's acting-out did with Lu? Bob Sendle's more nuanced reaction to Greg at the crime scene may have come from his own upbringing. Having lost his mom when he was nine and then being sent to an orphanage, Sendle knew something about boys and how they reacted to a mother's death.

Cold case prosecutor Ann Tomsic has a son. Her perspective on Greg was an indictment of Duane. What parent sends his thirteen-year-old boy upstairs to check his room if he thinks his house was burglarized? Because Greg was with Duane when Betty's body was found, Tomsic thought he knew more about that day than he told the police.

17. Scripts

manuscript: B n 1: A book, document, etc. written by hand; **2:** A person's (style of) handwriting

script: n 5c Psychol. The social role or behavior appropriate to particular situations that an individual absorbs through cultural influences and association with others.
—*The New Shorter Oxford English Dictionary*

There is no description of the crime and what [Duane Frye] saw. Captain Moomaw stated that his opinion is that this information was omitted because the author already knew the questions and answers.
—Progress Report | Investigator Bruce Isaacson, 2005

Shortly after he found Betty's body in 1973, Duane gave the cops a written statement. It is printed but barely legible, contains three sets of parentheses, and is riddled with cross-outs, misspellings, and inserts. It refers to Betty as "my wife," and his sons as "oldest" and "younger." The only person named is daughter Lynn, spelled as both "Marilyn" and "Merilynn."

Duane's statement is 26 lines long. Seven lines recite his itinerary before he arrived in Boulder. (Chevron to check on his car, Safeway to buy charcoal lighter fluid, the liquor store for a six-pack, Cinderella City "to get some sunglasses because I had forgotten mine. I discovered [crossed out and changed to 'didn't'] miss them until I got to Hampden.")

The next six lines recount his visits to the karate studio and then to Doug's and my apartment. The following nine are spent on checking out wedding banquet rooms, having a snack at the Pancake House, and dropping Lynn off at her apartment in Boulder. Duane's statement ends with, "We then drove home where we found my wife & called the neighbors who immediately called the sherrifs. We arrived a little after 5:00 P.M."

In 2005, the cold case cops gave Duane's statement to their in-house expert, Brice Moomaw. Moomaw wasn't concerned with where Duane said he went or how many cross-outs, misspellings, or parentheticals he used. He focused on how balanced the statement was. To Moomaw, truthful statements devoted roughly equal space to before, during, and after the key event of discovering Betty's body. (Others think the ratio should be 20-60-20.) Deceptive statements tend to spend the fewest words on the key event and relegate it to the end.

Moomaw broke Duane's 26 lines into three chronological sections. The first 24 lines dealt with what happened *before* Duane found Betty. Five words described what happened *when* he found her. Two lines said what happened *after*. Moomaw diagrammed the key sentence:↑[*Before*] "we then drove home / where we found my wife [*During*] / & called the neighbors who immediately called the sheriffs." → [*After*]

Duane devoted almost his entire statement to before he found Betty and two lines to after. The key event—discovering his wife's body—was five words sandwiched between before and after clauses in the next to last sentence. He said nothing about how he found Betty, where she was, or what he saw. To Moomaw, the statement wasn't just deceptive. It was cold.

But Duane devoted 26 words—more than any other part of his alibi—to replacing his sunglasses. He changed "discovered" to "didn't" and specified when and where he realized his sunglasses were missing. Bob Sendle found a pair of clip-on Raybans in a garbage barrel at the crime scene, apparently dropped by the killer while he was filling it with loot. On that white hot day, Duane needed his shades.

Forensics have come a long way since 1973 and 2005. In 2019, text analyst Wendell Rudacille offered to put Duane's statement under his psycholinguistic lens.

18. Reading Between the Words

You have to read not just between the lines, but between the words.
—Wendell C. Rudacille

Wendell Rudacille is an investigator and polygraph examiner with the Howard County, Maryland Police Department. He has spent fifty years in law enforcement, has a Master of Science in Psychology, and has written a treatise on deception, memory, and text analysis. I read *Identifying Lies in Disguise* in 2013, when I got the Frye case files, to try to make sense of statements Duane and his kids made in 1973 and afterwards.

Rudacille has devised a psycholinguistic process to determine whether a statement is probably true or false. He breaks the oral or written text into clauses and phrases. Then he notes redundancies, changes in pronouns and adjectives, spatial gaps and overstressed letters, places where information is missing or was censored, and other criteria mined from hundreds of statements that have been confirmed as true or false.

Scoring this data on worksheets produces a density analysis for probable truth or deception.

In March 2019, I contacted Rudacille for permission to quote from his book. To my surprise and delight, he didn't just agree: He offered to analyze the written statement Duane made shortly after he discovered Betty's body. Duane's statement scored a VIRPD (Verbal Indicators Related to Probable Deception) density of 6.6, quite close to the 9.0 density for confirmed deceptive suspect statements.

Rudacille is disciplined. He is wary of external details and facts that might contaminate his analysis. (He didn't ask if I thought Duane was a psychopath until after he'd delivered his report.) Nor does he speculate. Instead of reading a suspect's mind, he tries to put himself into his or her head. But even working in the blind—without context, and based on Duane's words alone—he had no doubt Duane knew Betty was dead when he left their house that morning.

To Rudacille, four things in Duane's statement stood out: Duane used "my" with reference to Betty's car; his statement contained no emotion; he didn't react to finding her body; and he didn't mention Betty at all until he found her dead.

Language also changes when one's perception of reality shifts. When Duane talked about his sunglasses, his syntax changed. And when one tries to tell a coherent false story while suppressing the truth, knowledge of the offense can leak. In saying he was at the Chevron station "about 10:55 A.M." (or 10:35, depending on how his handwriting is interpreted), Duane may have thrown down a marker.

Here's what Rudacille didn't know.

For her 45th birthday that March, Duane had given Betty a second-hand Lincoln convertible. The car he brought to the Chevron station the morning she was murdered was hers, not his. Calling it "my car" supports Rudacille's conclusion that Duane already knew Betty was dead when he embarked on the odyssey recounted in his statement. But Duane's taking ownership of his wife's car before he legitimately could have known she was dead isn't the only reason the Chevron is significant.

At 8:30 that morning, when the eldest Frye daughter, Jan arrived at the house in Littleton, Betty was fixing breakfast. At 9:30, Jan and Greg followed Duane in Jan's car to the Chevron, where he dropped off Betty's car. (After giving Duane a ride home, Jan drove Greg to his karate lesson in Boulder.) Chevron mechanics recalled seeing Duane twice: at 9:30, when he dropped the Lincoln off, and at 11:40, when he returned to check up on it. But Duane said in his statement that he was also there at 10:55.

10:55 (or 10:35) opens an even bigger can of worms. Unlike "a little after 5:00 P.M.," when Duane came home to find Betty's body, it is specific to the minute. And it falls right between the time Betty was murdered and Duane answered the door to Greg's friend Bret.

In 1973, the coroner said Betty died at around noon. When she was attacked, she fell onto her left hand. The crystal face of the watch on her left wrist cracked, and the watch stopped at 10:03. Back then, a jeweler examined the watch and found no internal damage. Because it needed to be lubricated and cleaned, he thought it had been running intermittently, stopping and starting again, before Betty was killed.

Since 1973, how time of death is estimated hasn't changed much. But in 2006, cold case coroner Michael Doberson was hamstrung by deficiencies in the original autopsy report. The report didn't mention rigor or livor mortis, nor was Betty's body temperature recorded at the crime scene or the morgue. Luckily, Doberson had other evidence.

Doberson said Betty died at 10:30 a.m. at the latest. He based that on when she was last seen alive (by Randy Peterson around 10:15, shaking out her mop), and remnants of meat found in her stomach. A light meal can be partially digested and leave the stomach within an hour. Digestion stops at death, and Betty died within minutes of being attacked. The meat in her stomach told Doberson she died within an hour or two after breakfast.

The sunglasses are also telling. In his written statement, Duane's earlier stops are precise: "I went to the Chevron station to ask them when they would have my car finished. About 10:55 A.M. I then went to Safeway and bought a can of charcoal lighter. I then went to the liquor store in the old shopping center and bought a six-pack of beer." Even without taking into account the Rayban clip-ons found with the loot in the garage, the sunglasses hit a psycholinguistic trifecta.

In recounting their role in his itinerary that morning, Duane switched to past perfect, fuzzed up the adjective, and changed his explanation mid-phrase: "I then went to Cinderella City to get some sunglasses because I had forgotten mine. I [discovered crossed out] didn't miss them until I got to Hampden [Avenue]."

Duane doesn't say he actually bought sunglasses. But his chatty explanation about why he needed them strikes a welcome note in his flat recitation, and Hampden and Cinderella City sound reassuringly specific. The problem is Cinderella City. When it opened in 1968, it was the largest covered shopping center west of the Mississippi. Its five malls had 250 stores and drew 15,000 visitors a day. On a summer weekend in 1973, it was so crowded you couldn't find a place to park.

19. Internal Editors

edit verb 1. Prepare (written material) for publication by correcting, condensing, or otherwise modifying it · remove unnecessary or inappropriate words, sounds, or scenes from a text, movie, or radio or television program.
—*dictionary.com*

Anything written or said is subject to an internal editor.
—**Wendell C. Rudacille | *Identifying Lies in Disguise***

Editors have a tough job. They look at narrative cohesion and flow, search for transitions and gaps, parse grammar, and polish prose. Editing a liar is even harder. But a liar need not engage a freelancer or a pro. His editor is in his head.

Forensic statements can be written or oral. Statement analyst Wendell Rudacille notes important differences between the two. Speech is spontaneous; writing presents a greater opportunity to rehearse. But in either case, the words are first uttered by an "inner voice." Rudacille calls this voice the internal editor. The internal editor's job depends on the communication mode.

Before committing words to paper, a written liar and his internal editor silently and privately converse. The liar's editor's first job is to prevent incriminating information from escaping the pen. After censoring guilty words and phrases, the editor must then combine new ones into sentences that tell a coherent story. Based on the misspellings, inserts, parentheticals, and cross-outs in Duane's 1973 written statement, his internal editor was working overtime.

Oral interviews are face to face. The spoken liar's editor can't cross out or erase words or phrases, and because the interviewer expects answers in real time, there is less opportunity to edit or rehearse. But liars need feedback to adapt. As forensic linguist Isabel Picornell says in *Analysing Deception in Written Witness Statements*, the constant feedback provided by the back-and-forth of an oral interview enables a liar to adapt his approach.

Written statements are more stressful than oral ones for other reasons, too. Picornell notes that if a suspect volunteers to write a statement, he can no longer remain silent. And, instead of being directed to a questioner who is present, a written statement is addressed to no one. The writer can't control who will read it. He must deceive a faceless multitude, not just the cop across the table.

20. Fight or Flight

Fight-or-flight is a physiological reaction in response to a perceived harmful event, attack, or threat to survival.
—*Wikipedia*

One minute the guy says, you know, things like, "I can keep a grudge for a long time," or something of this nature, to me, and the next minute he is like he is on some type of sedative, you know; the guy shows no emotion.
—Lieutenant Bob Sendle | Arapahoe County Grand Jury 1973

What are you doing here? Six women were killed at that time in Arapahoe County. As far as I'm concerned, that gives you a black mark.
—Duane Frye | Interview by Investigators Bruce Isaacson and Marv Brandt 2006

Being questioned by cops is scary for anyone. To a deceptive person, it is a threat to survival. Fight means confronting the questioner; flight is escaping through evasion or lies. But some escape routes are easier than others. According to statement analyst Wendell

Rudacille, it is less anxiety-provoking to use verbal evasion and linguistic loopholes than it is to tell a direct lie.

In a police interview, the threat isn't a gun. It's the questions. To survive, the suspect faces what Rudacille calls a two-pronged pitchfork. He must lie or suppress his guilt about two things: his role in the crime and how he answers the questions. How much he lets himself say depends on his personality, intelligence, and background; how guilty he feels about the crime; how worried he is about getting caught; how well he can blank out what he did; how guilty he feels about lying; how smoothly he can lie; how effectively he can rationalize his guilt; and how he views the questioner. Like a chameleon, the liar quickly adapts.

Duane made three statements: a written one at the scene in 1973, an oral one at his formal interview at the Sheriff's Office days later, and an oral one in response to cold case cops who came to his home in Florida without warning in 2006. In the intervening 33 years, some things had changed. But others had not.

Duane's parents owned thriving businesses in the center of Atwood, the Rawlins County seat in northwest Kansas. Duane himself had an engineering degree from CU, and his kids called him "Mr. Work the Problem." But in October 1972, after sixteen years specializing in efficiency and production problems at Martin Marietta, he was laid off.

In June 1973, when Betty was murdered, he was trying to launch two start-ups. By 2006, he lived in a gated community off a golf course with his second wife, Barbara. During the intervening years, Duane's personality had not changed, and he still had a lot to lose. But a suspect's anxiety level and what he expects also depend on the setting in which his statement is made.

Duane's written statement at the crime scene was made under Defcon 1: the deputy coroner had verbally Mirandized him, the printed form contained a Miranda warning, his statement was made in front of and formally witnessed by two cops, his first sentence confirmed it was voluntary ("I Herbert D. Frye who reside at... make this statement voluntarily"), and his wife's body lay just feet away in the garage. There are misspellings, inserts, and cross-outs, and the most detailed part of his alibi went to replacing his sunglasses. At the end ("we then drove home where we found my wife"), Duane's handwriting dramatically changed: the "v" in "drove" is over-stressed and there is a big gap between it and "where we found my wife." The "my" is so tiny it looks like it's trying to flee the page.

Three days later, Duane brought Leonard Davies, an experienced criminal defense lawyer, with him to his formal interview at the Sheriff's Office. Assistant District Attorney Jim DeRose asked Duane to take a polygraph. On Davies's advice, he refused. By then, his alibi had solidified and expanded; his stops the morning of the murder had doubled from four to eight.

But when Bob Sendle asked him what Betty was like, Duane turned combative. An adult who acted like a juvenile, he said. A spoiled brat. I put up with it for eight or ten years. Why would I kill her? Instead of denying he killed his wife, Duane offered up a rationale for believing he was innocent.

In Florida in 2006, cold case cop Marv Brandt remembered Duane sizing up him and Bruce Isaacson at the door. Were they smart, or Barney Fife? Concluding they'd be easy to fool, Duane invited them in. He immediately went on the offensive about supposed unsolved crimes in Arapahoe County at the time Betty was killed and told them only what he wanted them to know. He positioned himself at his dining room table so he could watch his second wife Barbara through the opening to the kitchen, where she chatted with a Florida cop.

But whatever Duane had managed to rationalize or tried to blank out, three decades did not erase his fear of Bob Sendle. That man was out to kill me, he told Isaacson and Brandt. Who? Brandt asked. The investigator who testified in court, Duane said. The demon he couldn't outrun.

21. Miller's Law

Miller's Law: In order to understand what a person is telling you, you must first accept that what the person has said is the complete truth, and then ask yourself: What is it true of?
—Wendell C. Rudacille | *Identifying Lies in Disguise*

I think they came into the house to steal guns. She was doing laundry, probably downstairs, pressing and changing clothing from a storage area, and was walking upstairs to get more clothes to take back into the basement storage area. And they were stealing things when she walked in on them. That's when she got killed.
—Duane Frye | 2006

Harvard psychologist George A. Miller was a pioneer in cognitive science. The psycho-linguistic rule named after him also makes biological sense. Because evasion and concealment require less energy and produce less anxiety than out-and-out lies, a liar is more likely to tell the truth about some things than to lie about everything. But if every lie contains at least a grain of truth, what truth is he trying to hide? And how will it leak out?

Liars aren't the only ones who combine fact and fiction to craft a convincing story.

Novelists spin plots from real-life experience, and they steal traits from relatives and friends. According to Rudacille, liars, too, sandwich unprovable assertions between facts to create "implied truth" and increase the "truth sale value" of their words. But the difference between liars and novelists isn't process or intent. Fiction writers want their stories to ring true, but they don't sell them as truth.

More sophisticated liars (Rudacille calls them "manipulative sociopaths") construct plausible-sounding hypotheticals to appeal to the interviewer's rationality and to emotionally distance themselves from the crime. Drawing from psychologist Virginia Satir, Rudacille calls this going into "computer mode." But the subconscious leaks from fabricated stories too.

When Duane was interviewed by cold case cops in 2006, he presented a detailed hypothetical of how his wife could have been killed in a burglary gone wrong. The key elements were guns, multiple intruders, and laundry. On its face, each assertion is plausible.

Duane owned $7,000 to $10,000 worth of rifles and shotguns. The Saturday morning of the murder, he and Betty were cleaning house. Linens were stripped from beds and bunched together. And there could have been more than one intruder: the loot was wiped clean of prints and bore signs that someone had worn gloves.

The problem isn't those elements. It is the house itself.

The Frye house was fifty feet wide and thirty feet deep. Entering the front door, one immediately faced stairs going up to the second floor and down to the basement. A narrow hallway ran past the stairs, to the kitchen on the left and a powder room on the right. Past the powder room lay the utility room and the walk-through door to the garage, where the loot and Betty's body were found. To get to the garage, one had to go through the utility room. The floor plan gave no room to maneuver—the distances were short, and the space was tight.

Duane hypothesized that Betty was doing laundry, moving back and forth between the second floor, the utility room on the first floor, and the basement. Clocks and appliances were looted from the kitchen and upstairs bedrooms. Travelling the same path, how could she and a burglar—not just one, but two—not immediately encounter each other? And how did she end up in the garage?

Duane's prized possessions were his guns. He didn't lock his doors, but he locked his guns in a cabinet in the basement. The cabinet wasn't a display case; he'd made it out of ¾ inch particle board and spray- painted it grayish white. The cabinet's padlock and hasp were intact, and the guns were untouched. Entering the basement, burglars might think there'd be guns from the reloading equipment nearby. But why bother taking cheap appliances if they came to steal guns? And how would they know Duane owned guns?

Miller's Law requires you to accept a statement as true, and then ask what it's true of—the subconscious leak. Duane valued his guns enough to speculate that multiple burglars would break into his home to steal them. Was Betty doing laundry when she was killed? The only person who would know that was her killer.

Collateral Damage

22. The Gap

To screenwriting guru Robert McKee, the essence of story is the gap between what we expect to happen when we act, and what really occurs.
—**Robert McKee | *Story: Substance, Structure, Style, and the Principles of Screenwriting***

You tell a joke and nobody laughs. At a party, the person you're chatting with looks past you for the door. Gap moments can be big or small, but when fantasy and reality collide, you want the earth to open underneath your feet. Gaps are the writer's holy grail, not (just) because humiliating your characters is entertaining, but because once you experience the gap, you cannot go back.

Murder cracks the gap wide open.

Betty's funeral was held at a tiny church in the Kansas cornfields. The night before, Duane had gathered his kids at a relative's house. Listen to the priest tomorrow, he told us. That's how I want you to remember her. Betty came from a big family, and the church was packed with family and friends. But the priest himself seemed not to know her. The only personal thing he said about Betty was that despite her problems, she managed to be kind.

Back home after the funeral, Duane invited Doug and me to dinner at The Red Lion Inn west of Boulder—to share memories of Betty, he said, including some that Doug may not have remembered or ever even knew. After the coldness of her funeral, Doug hungered for such memories.

Dinner started well. Remember when you were small? Duane began. But Duane didn't care about Doug's memories. She was sick, he said. She couldn't take care of you kids. I had to leave my job to watch you. I could have invested in Holubar. You have any idea how much I could've made investing in Holubar fifteen years ago? And that's not the only opportunity I lost because of her.

On and on he went. The jobs that were beneath him, the companies where he'd had an inside track, the career he could have had. Sometime in the middle of it all, I noticed he'd stopped wearing his wedding ring. I didn't want more kids after your sisters, he told Doug. If it had been up to me, you never would have been born.

A week or so later, Duane was arrested. After that, things moved fast—a grand jury, lawyers, the bail hearing. But that night at The Red Lion Inn was when Doug began to change.

My brother called Doug that golden ear of corn; he'd caught the Kansas in him but missed the innocence. After The Red Lion Inn, Doug's innocence was gone.

23. Heroes and Villains

In life, there are no essentially major or minor characters. Everyone is necessarily the hero of his own life story.
—**John Barth**

My brother is a damn sociopath.
—**Cherrie Otto, 2005**

When I wrote *Quiet Time,* most of what I had was memories. I'd talked to Betty the morning she was killed, seen Duane shortly afterwards, and was married to their son for the next nine years. I wrote the novel to try to understand what had happened and put it to rest. But the one place *Quiet Time* didn't go was into the fictional killer's head.

In July 1973, on a hot Saturday morning, Doug posed with his father for a wedding photo in front of the Boulder Unitarian Church. At first glance, they're strikingly alike: fair eyes, fair hair, fair skin. Slim-cut gray suits accentuated their similar wiry builds. But there the likenesses end.

Doug, with his whole life ahead of him, looks wary,

sullen, and lost. Duane appears carefree, grinning, hands clasped loosely behind his back, his hair combed neatly from an unlined brow. He'd just been indicted for beating his wife to death.

When the cold case cops came to Duane's door in Florida in 2006, he was 80 years old. To him, the years had been kind; their only marks were stubble on a balding head and deep furrows in his brow. His sister Cherrie had told the cops about his explosive temper. She was still afraid of him until the day she died.

Throughout the interview, Duane kept the upper hand. Evasive and belligerent, he said he didn't want to talk. But each time the cops rose to leave, he said, Go ahead and ask me more. When questioned about the crime, he changed the subject, said he wouldn't talk anymore about it or that he might need a lawyer. Yet time after time, he kept the interview going.

24. Text and Subtext

Text is the sensory surface of a work of art—what people see, say, and hear. Subtext is the life hidden beneath the surface.
—**Robert McKee** | *Story: Substance, Structure, Style, and the Principles of Screenwriting*

A: So I decided, well, maybe something had happened; that [Betty] had been called out of town and couldn't find me. About a quarter of 8:00, why, or 10 till 8:00, I decided to call back to their house again. And I called back and rang the phone eight or 10 times and Mr. Frye answered the phone. He said, "Duane Frye." And he— should I tell them what he said?

Q: Yes, go ahead.

A: Well, he said—I asked him if Betty was there and he said, no, that they had lost Betty over the weekend. And it was sort of a funny statement. I said, "What did you say?" And he said, "We lost Betty over the weekend." And I asked him what happened. And he said, "We think she ran head on into burglars."
—**Virginia Moldenhauer** | **Arapahoe County Grand Jury 1973**

Betty Frye and Virginia Moldenhauer were secretaries at Martin Marietta. In February 1973, four months before the murder, they started carpooling to work.

The second week of June was Betty's turn to drive. That Monday, she didn't show up. Virginia tried calling her house. When Betty's car wasn't in the company lot, she grew even more concerned. She called again and Duane told her Betty had run into burglars.

The previous Saturday, around 9:00 a.m. on the day Betty was killed, Virginia had gone to the Frye house to return a thermos Betty had left in her car. Duane came to the door in dark trousers and a dark print shirt, and maybe a necktie.

A week later, he called Virginia at work. What did you tell the cops about my clothes? he demanded. Was my shirt plaid or plain? Why did you tell them I was wearing a tie? And wasn't it 8:00 a.m. when you came over? Duane warned Virginia not to tell anyone he called. She promptly notified Martin Marietta security.

Days after the murder, Duane also went to the home of Bret Wacker, the boy who'd placed him at the scene of the crime at about the time it was committed. Are the cops questioning neighbors? he asked. Bret's mother felt threatened.

Duane's contacts with her and Virginia Moldenhauer sped up his arrest. But I keep coming back to how he described his wife's death to her distraught friend.

Betty didn't get lost over the weekend. And she didn't run head-on into anything.

She was struck from behind—maybe ambushed—and bludgeoned to death. Virginia thought it was sort of a funny statement. Maybe she read the subtext.

25. Works in Progress

work in progress: an unfinished work that is still being added to or developed.
—*dictionary.com*

---

rogue/1 An idle vagrant, a vagabond. **2** A dishonest or unprincipled person; a rascal. **5** An elephant or other large wild animal driven away or living apart from the herd and having savage or destructive tendencies.
—*The New Shorter Oxford English Dictionary*

Every tale needs a rogue. Some defenses need rogue cops.

Jim Blake was a cop. During his twenty years on the NYPD, Blake developed expertise in identifying infants' footprints by fishing dead babies out of the East River from a police launch.

Later, he retired to Colorado. Duane's defense lawyers hired him as their investigator. Blake's detailed investigatory report survives in the form of a running tab to defense counsel. His first task was to verify Duane's alibi for the Saturday when Betty was killed.

Because Betty died between 10:30 a.m. and noon, and

the clocks left in the garage stopped at 11:22, 11:23, and 11:27 a.m., Duane's whereabouts during that ninety-minute period were crucial.

Duane's story continued to evolve. By the time Blake entered the scene, it was even more jam-packed: spring cleaning with Betty, two trips to the Safeway, two runs to a nearby Chevron to check on the lube job for her car, a trip to a liquor store for beer, and a visit to mega-mall Cinderella City to inspect a sport coat for son Greg to wear to Doug's and my wedding, followed by a spur-of-the-moment hour-long drive to Boulder, where Duane said he stopped at our apartment before going to the karate studio, at which I saw him at 1:30 p.m.

Blake quickly ran into problems. Around 11:30 a.m., Greg's friend Bret had rung the Frye doorbell, and Duane answered the door. Blake initially tried to get around this by claiming Bret arrived an hour earlier. When Bret's story checked out, Blake had to account for Duane being home when Bret rang the bell. To do so, he added an 11:40 a.m. trip back from the Chevron for Duane to toss his own jacket in the front hall closet—not perfect, but close enough. But this required a third trip to the Chevron station and back in a very small window of time, and more changes still.

Now Duane had to leave for Cinderella City at noon, depart the mall at 12:15 p.m., and arrive at the karate studio at 1:05. When the only witnesses Blake could find were a liquor store clerk and mechanics who saw Duane on his first two Chevron trips, Blake shrugged off the rest of Duane's alibi and canceled a planned ride-along as "NOT NECESSARY."

The carpenters on the roof cater-corner to the Fryes had seen an old green pickup parked in front of the Frye house the day of the murder. No neighbors reported seeing any strange vehicles, but an official search was launched. Bob Sendle sent a teletype describing the truck to every law enforcement agency within 150 miles, and cops photographed trucks throughout Arapahoe County. A 12-year-old boy who lived across the street from the Fryes saw the pickup too. The DA told Blake the owner lived down the block, but Blake discounted that because criminals don't usually commit crimes in their own neighborhood.

Blake's contributions to the defense didn't end there. After the cops officially cleared the crime scene, Blake claimed he found latent glove impressions, a pinkie print, and three partial palm prints inside the Frye house. Why gloves *and* fingerprints? There must have been two intruders, of course! Blake convinced prosecutors to give him the print charts of two would-be burglars in custody at the county jail so he could compare them to the latents he'd found. Bingo—a match!

Blake later claimed the cops confirmed the ID, but he never gave them his set of prints. In 1974, after they'd dismissed the case, the DA's office asked Duane's lawyers for the prints in order to make their own comparison. But by then, the prints Blake claimed he found had disappeared. In 2005, the cold case cops were still looking for them.

How did Blake get away with this? Maybe, as DA Gallagher told me in 1994, because we didn't investigate cases then the way we do now. Like Blake's report, the DA's case was a work in progress; 1973 court filings show a revolving and growing cast of Assistant District Attorneys assigned. With the aggressive defense Duane's lawyers mounted, it was easier for the DA to throw Bob Sendle under the bus than go to trial.

In 1974, Blake bought property in Idaho Springs, an old mining town near Colorado's first big gold strike. He claimed his stake had a vein of gold twelve inches wide. In 1986, he died in a place called Squirrel Gulch. In 2005, Duane's new lawyers moved to dismiss the cold case on grounds that Blake was essential to his defense. The motion was denied.

26. The Ballad of Tom Gussie

I met her on the mountain, there I took her life
Met her on the mountain, stabbed her with my knife
—**The Kingston Trio** | *The Ballad of Tom Dooley*

Defense lawyer Gary Lozow recommends that investigators look in another direction that evidence had pointed to then and now: to Thomas Gussie, a convicted burglar.

Gussie, who died in 2000 at the age of 48, left fingerprints at the house and a witness who was shingling a roof on the street identified him visiting the house that day, Lozow said. Gussie moved to California shortly after the murder in 1973 and was soon convicted of a very similar burglary in which he was caught piling possessions in a garage, he said.

Gussie had a drug-and-violence background, Lozow said. He was a man of the streets.
—*The Denver Post* | **October 26, 2008**

The Kingston Trio's *Ballad of Tom Dooley* hit #1 on the Billboard chart in 1958. Based on an old folk tune about a Civil War-era murder, the song posed a tragic triangle of Tom, his lover Laura Foster, and a sheriff named Grayson who hauled Tom in for killing Laura.

But history reveals another triangle: Tom, Laura, and Ann Melton, the woman Tom had been sleeping with since he was 12. Some locals believed Ann killed Laura, and that Tom went to the gallows for Ann. In *Lift Up Your Head, Tom Dooley*, North Carolina historian John Foster West tells an even grittier tale.

When rebel soldier Tom Dula (Dooley) returned to the hill country after the war, he took up not just with Ann and Laura, but also with their cousin Pauline. Pauline gave Tom syphilis, and he in turn gave it to Ann and Laura. Tom blamed Laura for infecting him. Perhaps egged on by Ann, he lured Laura to her death on the mountain by promising to marry her. At trial, Pauline was the star witness against Tom. In 1866 and 1958, a love triangle was sexier than syphilis.

Like Tom Dooley, Tom Gussie was remade for an audience.

Gussie's first run-in with the law was for stealing ice cream from the back of a truck. When he was 18, he took the rap for his kid brother on a marijuana charge. Four days after his 21st birthday, and six weeks after Betty's murder, he and a young sidekick were nabbed trying to break into Georgia Boys, a burger joint a mile and a half from the Frye house. They were taken to the Arapahoe County Jail.

Defense investigator Blake seized the moment.

Claiming he'd found prints at the house, he talked the DA into giving him Gussie's prints to compare. Blake was the only one who ever saw the prints he said he'd found, or claimed they matched Gussie's. By the time the DA asked Blake for his set, they'd disappeared.

Randy Peterson, the carpenter on the roof cater-corner to the Fryes, described the man in Duane's backyard as five-nine, with a slim build and dark hair. Blake told the cops the man Peterson saw was blond and five-eleven. In 1973, Gussie was five-eleven, blond, and 175 pounds. Peterson later said the man he'd seen was in his late twenties or thirties. (He also remembered Blake as a retired New York cop who was easygoing and fair. Blake told him Duane and Betty had been having problems but were working things out.)

Gussie agreed to be polygraphed regarding Betty's murder. The test was scheduled for December 1973. There is no record of the results, but his sidekick took a polygraph and passed. Neither of them was ever charged in Betty's murder, or even for the Georgia Boys caper.

The "very similar burglary" Lozow fed *The Den er Post* occurred in Sacramento, California 17 years after Betty was murdered. Gussie climbed through an unlocked window of an empty house, offered no resistance when caught, and never denied what he'd done. The eagle tattooed on his chest and the Pink Panther stamp on his arm, the mug shots with hollow eyes and sunken cheeks, the rap sheet for careless driving, failed burglaries, and DUIs, tell not the drugs-and-violence tale of a man of the streets, but a non-violent alcoholic's life of petty crime.

Disabled and suffering mild brain damage from a motorcycle accident, Gussie returned to Colorado to live with the brother for whom he'd taken the marijuana rap 30 years earlier. In 2000, when he died of cirrhosis, the responding officer reported that Gussie's brother wept.

The Right Man

27. The Right Man

In *A Criminal History of Mankind,* Colin Wilson recounts what happened when Sergei Aksakov's grandfather ("this noble, magnanimous, often self-restrained man") became enraged at his daughter. His elderly wife threw herself at his feet and begged for pity on the girl. He grabbed his wife by the hair and dragged her around the house until he was too exhausted to continue. He fell into a deep sleep, and the next morning woke up in a good mood, asking for his tea.

Wilson writes, "In this one area of his life, his control over his family, he has made the decision to be out of control. It is provoked by his daughter persisting in a lie. This infuriates him; he feels she is treating him with lack of respect in assuming he can be duped. So he explodes and drags his wife around by the hair. He feels no shame later about his behavior; his merriness the next morning shows that his good opinion of himself is unaffected. He feels he was *justified* in exploding, like an angry god."

Wilson calls him The Right Man.

Duane has a free temper. In other words, he has a temper three or four minutes and then all of a sudden everything is fine, you know. But yet he is a very, very non-emotional type of individual. "I put up with it for

eight or ten years," he said. "I had no reason to kill her."
—Lieutenant Bob Sendle | Arapahoe County Grand Jury 1973

Doug and his sister Lynn remembered the night their dad threw a glass of milk at the wall. Betty had served beans for dinner, and beans made Duane fart.

Duane got so angry at other drivers that his sister Cherrie wouldn't ride in his car.

Cherrie's ex-husband Hank recalled Duane exploding at a party and berating Betty in front of a roomful of guests. These are my guests, he said. You will treat them right!

Duane was the only relative Betty's nephews feared. But kids are impressionable, and everyone loses his temper.

One of the last times I saw Betty was on Mother's Day 1973. At dinner, she was cold and distant. I was surprised when, doing the dishes later, she confided in me. Duane had exploded at a woman from the telephone company. Betty was worried for him, not for herself. Three weeks later, she was dead.

The court files tell what happened, but not why. *The Diagnostic and Statistical Manual of Mental Disorders, 5th Edition (DSM-5)* lays out a smorgasbord of intermittent explosive disorder, repressed rage, pathological narcissism, and narcissistic personality disorder.

These diagnoses seem generic, somehow incomplete. They catch the rage but miss the after-effect—the everything-being-fine-later, that losing control can be a conscious and selective choice.

And that the Right Man's flashpoint is his wife.

28. The Right Man, Part 2

When a Right Man finds a woman who seems submissive and admiring, it deepens his self-confidence, fills him with a sense of his own worth. His problem is lack of emotional control and a deep-seated sense of inferiority; so success cannot reach the parts of the mind that are the root of the problem.
—**Colin Wilson** | *A Criminal History of Mankind*

The Right Man is as old as time. The Greeks knew him as Hubris, whose arrogance and lack of restraint affronted the gods. The Old Testament speaks of pride going before destruction and a haughty spirit before a fall.

But the bible on the Right Man was written by twentieth-century Canadian novelist A.E. Van Vogt. Researching male aggression for a thriller he planned to write, Van Vogt noted a pattern in certain highly dominant men. In *A Report on the Violent Male*, he describes a boy whose father is detached, missing, or overly strict with his son, and a mother who becomes the boy's "ally- antagonist," a role women will replay throughout his life.

If a woman challenges or crosses him, a Right Man

withdraws in smoldering resentment and then erupts into rage. But his dependence on and need to control his woman dooms him: If she leaves him, *he* must die.

Van Vogt used this research for his 1962 novel, *The Violent Man.* Its protagonist, Seal Ruxton, is an American expatriate accused of espionage and being held in a Communist Chinese prison camp. A flashback recounts his marriage in the States. After his wife was incapacitated by a car accident, she was raped. Ruxton blamed her for becoming "spoiled goods," but when she left him, he fell deathly ill: "We're the kind of men who can't have a woman leave us," he explains.

At the prison camp, Ruxton clashes with another Right Man, the commandant. When he has an affair with the commandant's wife and she catches him in a lie, Ruxton's rage builds: "If she turns against me, I'll pay her back if it's the last thing I do." Rage confers a murderous power. But once the storm passes, Ruxton continues to burn.

The Right Man has other names now. What sets him apart from the garden-variety toxically masculine male, however, is his dependence on a woman he idealizes and must destroy. The Right Man's paradox and downfall is that he can't live without her.

Betty was gorgeous—a svelte blonde, a standout. Duane's sister Cherrie said he was attracted to Betty's physical perfection. But her death didn't quench his anger. After her funeral, he bitterly recounted the opportunities she cost him and said she'd tricked him into conceiving his sons.

Previously in good health, Duane needed a coronary bypass and the removal of his gallbladder soon after Betty's murder.

After the charges against him were dropped, he began dating a former neighbor, Barbara Dean. Barb was dowdy and wore glasses. She liked to send little gifts and Hallmark cards, and when she was excited, she clapped her hands. Cherrie Otto and Betty's sister, Jean Brickell, were flabbergasted when Duane married her six months later. And by the time the cold case rolled around, Barb was a slim, stylish blonde.

29. Inciting Incidents

An inciting incident radically upsets the balance in the protagonist's life.

—Robert McKee | *Story: Substance, Structure, Style, and the Principles of Screenwriting*

I talked with Teri Vogt at Arapahoe County Sheriff's Office in regard to her friend who knows the FRYE family. She said that her friend is her boyfriend's mother, last name of KREBS. Teri said that she was with them at the Holly Inn South on Friday night 6-8-73 when they accidently ran into the FRYE's and her impression was that MRS. FRYE was a friendly, warm, outgoing person. Teri said she was not introduced to MR. FRYE and he stayed in the background and didn't say anything. Teri said she would try to get in touch with MRS. KREBS and arrange for us to talk with her.

—Investigator Louis J. Lajoie | Progress Report 1973

If Louis Lajoie followed up with Midge Krebs in 1973, there's no record of it. But Midge, pushing 90 and still sharp, resurfaced in the cold case. In 2006, investigators interviewed her in Texas.

As Lajoie had reported, the night before Betty was

murdered, Midge ran into her and Duane at a Mexican restaurant called The Holly Inn. A third person was with them: Barbara Dean, a close family friend whose husband Jim worked with Duane at Martin Marietta. Midge said Betty seemed sweet, quiet, but not particularly happy that night. She acknowledged talk in 1973 that Duane and Barb had been seeing each other before the murder.

Midge had more to say to Betty's sister, Jean. She told Jean that Duane and Barb were sitting next to each other in a booth that Friday night, giggling and having drinks, while Betty watched from across the table. As Midge watched Betty, she had the sense Betty was suddenly putting two and two together. Jean and the cold case cops think Betty confronted Duane about Barb that night.

Midge's suspicions tally with the grand jury testimony of Duane's sister Cherrie in 2006. According to Cherrie, Duane told their mother that Betty began crying uncontrollably that Friday night. On Saturday morning, she was still crying. Hours later, she was dead.

Time gives gossip the weight of truth. But something always lights the match. And must an inciting incident be rational?

A 1973 police report contains this detail. When cops arrived at the Frye house the day of the murder, a patrolman was assigned to record motorists who approached or passed by more than once. The second name on his list, at 5:59 p.m., was Barbara Dean. She identified herself as a family friend before parking and going to the door. Diligent as he was, it wasn't the cop's job to ask how she knew Betty was dead. If Barb gave an explanation, he didn't note it.

30. Ally-Antagonists

ally/2 collect. Kindred, relatives; associates, confederates.
—*The Shorter Oxford English Dictionary*

---

antagonist/1 An opponent, an adversary; an opposing force.
—*The Shorter Oxford English Dictionary*

Lolita wouldn't have liked anybody Duane married, because nobody was good enough. The only person Lolita would approve of being married to Duane was herself.
—Cherrie Otto | 2015

I was sitting next to Duane and his mother. I wasn't even really part of the conversation, except in a polite way. I recall her saying that it was going to be different with Stephie and Doug, and I don't recall why, but that it would be easier. I had some impression that he might be seeing somebody else, or that he might know someone. In other words, it might be good if he saw somebody else.
—Lillian Shafer | 1998

In fiction, the most potent antagonist is someone who was once a friend. The betrayal lands like a sucker punch. If the antagonist was your BFF or ally-for-all-time, you're down for the count.

To Duane's mother Lolita, Betty and her family were Bohunks. Betty's sister Thelma said Lolita had a bitter tongue and could cut you with a remark. She and her mother went once to Lolita's gift shop in Atwood to pick out an engagement present for Lolita's daughter Shirley. I'm always curious how cheap people are when they buy a wedding gift, Lolita told them. Throughout her marriage to Duane, Lolita rode Betty mercilessly. At Betty's funeral, she wore a gay flowered dress.

Soon after Betty was murdered, Lolita rolled in from Kansas like a Sherman tank. People had brought turkey and ham to the Frye house, but she made the kids eat liverwurst. When Greg said he didn't like liverwurst, she said Betty had spoiled him.

A day or so later, my own mother flew to Denver. Doug and I took her on an outing to the foothills with Lolita and Duane.

Mom was tough, but even she fell under Duane's domineering spell. Years later, she told me he said things she would've hesitated or felt funny about saying herself, but that she thought he was *right* and she would have been wrong. What really struck her was the closeness between mother and son. Yet Lolita would turn out to be Duane's downfall.

The Right Woman

31. The Right Woman

recipe/1: PRESCRIPTION 2: a set of instructions for making something from various ingredients 3: a formula or procedure for doing or attaining something < a — for success>.
—*Merriam-Webster's Collegiate Dictionary, Eleventh Edition*

Don't ever ask him any questions; don't negate him or what he does, or tells you; put his comfort first, ahead of your own, ahead of the children. Don't bother him with your physical problems, and be available for his comfort even if you're in a state of nausea, or running a temperature of 104.
—**A. E. Van Vogt** | *A Report on the Violent Male*

He described his wife as an invalid type. I am not sure I am quite wording it right. An adult that acts like a juvenile or a, you know, a spoiled brat type situation.
—**Lieutenant Bob Sendle | Arapahoe County Grand Jury 1973**

My divorce from Doug left me with few of his family's mementos: two glazed mugs in which we'd mixed Tang and powdered Lipton's to make Betty's Russian tea; a cookie tin with packets of needles, spools of thread, and a pair of reindeer gamboling across the lid; and a small orange three- ring binder with a 1940s wasp-waisted woman silhouetted on the cover.

When a button came off, I used Betty's sewing box. Her mugs I stored in the back of my cupboard. But the binder was an orphan. Jammed into a shelf of cookbooks in my basement, *My Fa orite Recipes* over the years suffered a split spine and a cracked vinyl cover.

The woman on the cover wore a jaunty toque and apron with an extravagant bow. One hand perched saucily on her hip; the other balanced a platter of pastries with steam rising from the top. But *My Fa orite Recipes* wasn't just a recipe file. It was a domestic bible, a repository for ambitions and dreams.

Betty's binder was crammed with pamphlets for coconut animal cut-up cakes and buffet skillets and a brochure for china from Montgomery Ward. Recipes for dove and pheasant were sure to please her husband Duane, and she saved Joan Fontaine's menus for the dinner parties they'd throw. In peacock blue pencil and violet ink, she made notes—*More like sherbet*—next to the recipe for lemon ice bars.

On a blank page in the back, she sketched a rose garden and her sister Agnes's chrysanthemum bed. Betty's aspirations, refracted through the appliances she used, the dinnerware that caught her eye, the gardens she hoped to plant. And a recipe for disaster in a marriage to a man to whom she was irreparably flawed.

32. The Right Woman, Part 2

I think my mother did learn, sort of like Barb did, that you don't always say – like women do sometimes. You don't always say your whole opinion, because he's going to try to make you change your mind anyway, and it's not going to make any difference.
—Lynn Frye | Arapahoe County Grand Jury 1973

The second wife, Barbara, impressed me as being sort of a school marm type, clearly under the domination of Duane.
—Mark Shafer | 1998

Her house looked like a furniture store. The warmest room was the family room, where they had a bar. And that's because Jim Dean was behind it.
—Jean Brickell | 2011

On a Friday night in the spring of 1973, Jean and Dick Brickell threw a party on their back patio. Jean's younger sister Betty came with Duane, and Jim and Barb Dean were there too. Dick took a snapshot.

Betty offers up a glass of punch with one hand and

coquettishly cups her platinum bouffant with the other. The gestures draw you to her flowing sleeves and the sash cinching her tiny waist. In his untucked sport shirt with bold bandolier print, Duane flashes a bad-boy grin.

Jim Dean towers over them, smiling genially in his hornrims, pens peeking from the pocket of his short-sleeved dress shirt. His wife Barb sits at the picnic table. Her curls are prim and her dress is matronly, but she tried. Jean is the broad-shouldered sporty redhead in the pearls and coral sheath who's laughing into the camera. Duane isn't looking at Barb or Betty. He's looking at Jean.

Betty and Duane met at a country dance when she was a high school junior in Kansas. Betty had been dating his cousin, but somehow the partners switched and Jean found herself dancing with Duane. He kissed Jean on the cheek, and later she teased Betty that he'd kissed her first. Years later, when Betty was hospitalized and undergoing shock treatments, Duane came to Jean's house. I should have married you, he told her. You were the strong one.

Jim and Barb Dean met at the University of Illinois. She was President of the Accountancy Club; her roommates called her Babs and described her as a connoisseur of male photographs who buried herself in writing letters and themes. Jim belonged to a prestigious fraternity and the engineering honor society. At Martin Marietta, he became a helium expert vital to the Titan missile project.

In the early '60s, the Brickells, the Deans, and the Fryes were a close circle of young couples on their way up. Duane worked with Jim at Martin. Jim and Barb lived two doors down from him and Betty, and Dick and Jean bought a house on a street that dead-ended between them. They partied after work and went hunting together in Kansas.

But Duane used and betrayed Jim.

When Betty applied to Martin Marietta for a job, Jim was her reference. When Betty was murdered, Jim went to the mortuary to identify her. I'll regret it the rest of my life, he told Jean. It was the worst thing I ever saw.

Shortly after, when Barb said she was into the NOW (National Organization of Women) movement and needed to express herself, Jim was heartsick. She didn't take a stick of furniture when she left, he wailed to Dick, just her clothes. Why? When Dick told him Barb was marrying Duane, Jim said, I think I'll get my gun and kill him.

Jim returned to Illinois. He met a woman he wanted to marry, but he got cancer of the esophagus. He'd already lost his infectious laugh.

33. Causality

CAUSALITY drives a story in which motivated actions cause effects that in turn become the causes of yet other effects, thereby interlinking the various levels of conflict in a chain reaction of episodes to the Story Climax.
—**Robert McKee | *Story: Substance, Structure, Style, and the Principles of Screenwriting***

Impulsive actions and behaviors are only the final results of one's acting in accordance with his or her basic personality. What may seem, on the surface as an "impulsive" act, may have been imagined, fantasized, or mentally played out countless times over the person's lifespan.
—**Wendell C. Rudacille | *Identifying Lies in Disguise***

The central characteristic of The Right Man is the "decision to be out of control," in some particular area. We all have to learn self-control, to deal with the real world and other people. But with some particular person—a mother, a wife, a child—we may decide that this effort is not necessary and allow ourselves to explode. But this decision creates, so to speak, a permanent weak point in the boiler, the point at which it always bursts.
—**Colin Wilson | *A Criminal History of Mankind***

I put up with it for eight or ten years, he said. I had no
reason to kill her.

**—Lieutenant Bob Sendle | Arapahoe County Grand
Jury 1973**

DAs balk at cases in which a sane person commits a
spontaneously violent act. If he has no record of
violence and scant time to plan, how do they convince a
jury he intended to kill?

But violent rage and a conscious decision to be out of
control are linked. According to Colin Wilson, rage is
the predicate for the decision. The juxtaposition of two
apparently contradictory dynamics—on the one hand,
resentment and rage ("I put up with it"), and on the
other, a rational appraisal of his marital difficulties ("I
had no reason to kill her")—reflects the divide at the
very heart of The Right Man's nature.

But giving yourself permission to explode has a price: it
enslaves you to your emotions and creates a permanent
weak point in your boiler.

A killer who prizes control might fear he'll lose it again.
To master his impulses, he might be driven to examine
them. He might seek vindication in a philosophy. If he
had no interest in religion before, he might even join a
church.

Duane was so enthralled with libertarian author Ayn

Rand that he made his kids read *Atlas Shrugged*. Rand's philosophy is that the individual exists purely for his own sake. After Betty's murder, Duane turned to Science of the Mind Church. Like Rand's objectivism, Science of the Mind is more a pseudo-religion or philosophy than a real one; it is based not on the authority of any established belief, but on what it can accomplish for practitioners.

Duane became so wrapped up in its teachings that they were all he read. He dominated group meetings and was asked to leave.

In 2006, Duane was still trying to come to terms with his impulses. All anger and concern are based on fear, he told the cold case cops. Fear and frustration make a person do anything.

34. Criminality and Flow: Addiction, Anomie, and Alienation

When I took off for the second run, I was released as the full force and energy of who I am as a person. In a way, the second run was a perfect run. There are few times in our lives where we become the thing we're doing.
—**Andrea Lawrence | Olympic Skier**

Flow is the process of total involvement with life, when a person's body or mind is stretched to its limits in a voluntary effort to accomplish something difficult and worthwhile…. But when a person becomes so dependent on the ability to control an enjoyable activity that he cannot pay attention to anything else, then he loses the ultimate control: the freedom to determine the content of consciousness.
—**Mihaly Csikszentmihalyi |** *Flow: The Psychology of Optimal Experience*

anomie: personal unrest, alienation, and uncertainty that comes from a lack of purpose or ideals.
—*Merriam-Webster's Collegiate Dictionary, Eleventh Edition*

Sports psychology is all about flow. Andrea Lawrence was in flow when she won her second gold medal on that perfect run. Pro golfers so dread choking—the self-consciousness which destroys flow—that they won't even utter the word. But flow isn't just for pro athletes.

We've all had at least fleeting moments of being so into what we're doing that we lose track of time. Transcending the physical world becomes its own reward.

In *A Criminal History of Mankind*, Colin Wilson says criminals engage in violent acts because the physical stimulus enables them to feel alive in a way akin to being in flow. The sharpened awareness that danger produces makes crime addictive. Hungarian-American psychologist Mihaly Csikszentmihalyi warned in his book that flow-producing activities can also become addictive. But flow and crime are linked in yet another way.

Wilson believed the insights gained from intense creative focus eliminate the boredom of and dissatisfactions with life which give rise to the need to assert self-respect through criminal aggression. He even went so far as to claim that "no poet, artist, or composer has ever committed a calculated, first-degree murder." (Writers and novelists apparently sublimate their desires.)

Another way to transcend the physical world is to immerse oneself in the creative efforts of others. Books have long been a tool of prison reform. Fiction in particular provides a window into the minds and experiences of others, a way out of one's own head. Reading novels enables inmates to focus and helps engender a more complex world view. In teaching how others make sense of their lives, novels show there are other ways to respond to conflicts and pressures than the decisions that lead to criminal acts.

Duane Frye never read fiction. He thought it was a waste of time.

35. Motive

motivation/ 2: a motivating force, stimulus, or influence: INCENTIVE, DRIVE
—*Merriam-Webster's Collegiate Dictionary, Eleventh Edition*

Motive: The emotional, psychological, or material need that impels, and is satisfied by, a behavior.
—**Brent Turvey** | *Criminal Profiling: An Introduction to Behavioral Evidence Analysis*

Motive and intent both involve state of mind. They are, however, legally distinct. Intent is when you decide to use a particular means to accomplish an act. Motive is what makes you do it. DAs must prove intent. They don't have to prove motive, but because jurors are human, they want to know why someone does what they're accused of doing. In 1973 and 2006, prosecutors believed Duane had two motives for killing his wife: Barbara Dean, and Betty's life insurance.

Betty had two insurance policies with Martin Marietta: life insurance with a face value of $8,000 and a double indemnity accident clause, and a $100,000 accidental death policy. Duane was the sole beneficiary of both.

If he was 48 or older when she died, he also would receive $175 a month until age 62. Duane turned 48 exactly two weeks before Betty's murder. In 1973, Martin's insurance administrator estimated Duane's payoff at $149,000.

That's just short of a million dollars in 2023.

Attraction to another woman and being the sole beneficiary of a big insurance policy are rational motives for murder. Prosecutors believe they are far easier to sell to a jury than the complexities of a man who felt deceived by his wife and betrayed by a world that refused to recognize his primacy and worth.

In 1956, after working at four other companies as an industrial engineer specializing in efficiency and production problems, Duane went to work at Martin Marietta. Martin competitively ranked employees on a "totem pole." Duane's rank determined whether he was promoted from technical engineer to the increasingly responsible management positions to which he aspired. After Betty's murder, his co-workers painted a picture of a man who'd been struggling to maintain his grip.

Duane had been one of the first to volunteer to go to Huntsville, Alabama, to get Martin's Sky Lab off the ground. Less than a year later, he returned to the Denver-area plant. One colleague told the cops Duane was frequently frustrated and couldn't work with customers in Alabama.

Duane's always been outspoken, another said. He

couldn't hold his tongue; he'd have his say, then calm down and revert to his normal self. A third saw him angry a couple of times and said he was very intelligent but also very impatient and abrupt. In October 1972, seven months before Betty was murdered, Martin laid Duane off.

Duane framed entering private consulting as his decision, a time he could finally strike out on his own. If he was to succeed, he knew he had to work the problem of his interpersonal skills. So he enrolled in a Dale Carnegie course.

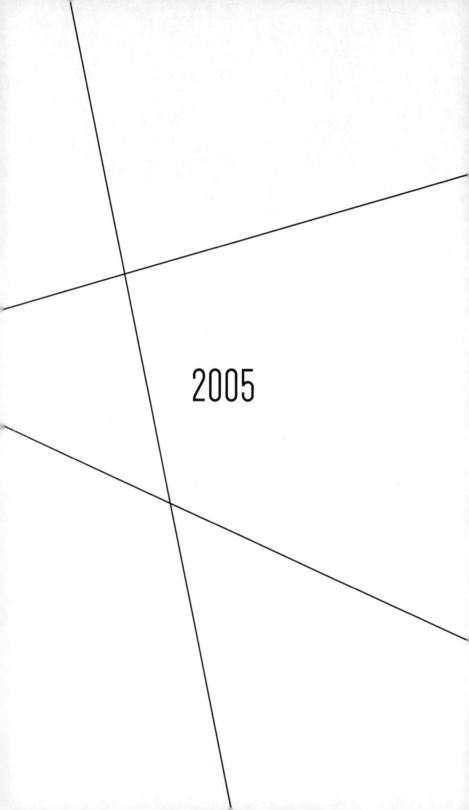

2005

36. Confessions

Confession: In literature, an autobiography, either real or fictitious, in which intimate and hidden details of the subject's life are revealed.
—*Encyclopedia Britannica*

Confession: In criminal law, a voluntary statement made by a person charged with the commission of a crime or misdemeanor, communicated to another person, wherein he acknowledges himself to be guilty of the offense charged, and discloses the circumstances of the act or the share and participation which he had in it.
—*Black's Law Dictionary*

Duane told Lolita he killed Betty. She [Lolita] told me three separate times. He said Betty was so upset about Doug and Stephanie getting married, and Stephanie being Jewish and Betty being so Catholic. She cried and cried. She wouldn't stop crying and he couldn't take it anymore. My brother is a damned sociopath.
—**Cherrie Otto | 2005**

There are often voice and words in a silent look.
—**Ovid**

In 2005, when Cherrie called, eighty-year-old Jean Brickell was gardening on her porch. Jean had always liked Cherrie; in the Frye family, she was a different breed of cat. She'd told Jean her mother Lolita had hated her, and her father was the only person who'd been good to her. But this time Cherrie wasn't calling to catch up. For years, she'd wanted to tell Jean that Duane had confessed.

Jean was in shock, but the confession rang true.

In 1973, she'd missed Duane's bail hearing, but her husband Dick had gone. When Duane was led into court in his orange jumpsuit, it wasn't the jail garb that struck Dick Brickell. It was the look on Duane's face. Oh my God, he's guilty, Dick told Jean. If he didn't do this, I'd be amazed. And back then, Jean had her own reasons to suspect Duane.

Their mother Cundy had wanted to see Betty's body. The coroner said he could fix Betty up, but Duane insisted on a closed casket. Then he said he didn't want to bury Betty in Denver because his kids didn't plan to stay in Colorado. Jean asked Cundy to bury her in the family plot in Kansas. He doesn't want any part of Betty, Cundy said. He doesn't even want her to be buried in her own parish.

About the time Cherrie called, Jean's son had been contacted by Howard Morton, head of Families of Homicide Victims and Missing Persons (FOHVAMP). Morton wanted to know if they were interested in reopening Betty's case. Now Jean called Morton and told him Duane had confessed. Morton e-mailed cold case cop Bruce Isaacson with a simple plea: Can you fry Frye?

For Duane's confession to stick, they needed Cherrie on tape.

At 11:30 a.m. on September 1, 2005, the Brickells pulled up to Piccolo's Italian restaurant in southeast Denver. Dick knew the owner; they'd be shown the quietest table. Isaacson had fitted them with audio monitoring and recording devices. Jean wore hearing aids, and the monitor that allowed Isaacson to communicate with them resembled a hearing aid, so she wore the monitor and Dick the recorder.

Isaacson followed in an unmarked car and parked in the lot. When the Brickells greeted their guest, a tiny, sparrow-like woman wearing heavy glasses, he switched his recorder on.

Guilt-ridden and determined to do the right thing, 76-year-old Cherrie didn't hesitate or equivocate. When she visited her mother in assisted living in 1995 or '96, Lolita had told her Duane killed Betty because she wouldn't stop crying. The next morning, she was still crying and he couldn't put up with it. Lolita was very happy when she recounted this.

Three or four months later, Cherrie asked her again. Yes, Lolita said, he did it. A few months later, Cherrie brought it up a third time. Lolita now didn't want to talk about it. You know how Duane is, she said. She was still crying and he…

Are you willing to help the police? Dick asked Cherrie.

Oh, yes, she said. Gladly.

37. Character Sketches

GENERAL ASSESSMENT QUESTIONS

63. What makes the subject angry?
Stupid people. Short fuse.

65. What days/dates are especially significant to the subject? (Birthdays, holidays, anniversaries, death of family member, etc.) Mother's Day—The most important holiday.

OTHER INFORMATION WHICH WOULD HELP IN UNDERSTANDING THE SUBJECT'S PERSONALITY:
When mother was moved from CA to CO due to nursing home requirement, [he] visited a lot and then got tired/bored and stopped going to see her much. Mom was a hobby and he got tired of it.
—Cherrie Otto | 2005

14. Did any family member have a great deal of influence in subject's life?
Mother was very partial to her first child and son.

77. How does subject react to the loss (by death, separation, alienation, etc.) of people important to him/her?
He did not show any emotion after my sister was murdered.

79. What is truly important to the subject?
Getting what he wants.
—Jean Brickell | 2005

---

61. Does the subject hold any particular prejudices?
Did not like Catholics (wife was Catholic), black people.

65. What events seem to shake subject's self-confidence?
When he couldn't "win" a discussion.
—Dick Brickell | 2005

When interviewing [Duane] explain to him the case will
not just "go away." His life from this point forward will
be miserable unless he deals with it now. He will always
wonder when authorities will be knocking on his door or
if he is being followed…. Remind him that [Betty] was
on medications for bipolar disorder. She took things too
seriously; specifically, Catholicism, Judaism, and
Stephanie's abortion. Her [Betty's] demeanor changed
during the marriage, which added stress to the whole
family. The marriage was not a good marriage.
[Minimize] that he is a cold-blooded killer. Describe the
case as manslaughter instead…. Never let [him] believe
he has any room to dispute the facts of the case or
[doubt] that the case will continue forward with or
without his input.

Investigator Bruce Isaacson | Progress Report 2006

Bruce Isaacson and Marv Brandt knew one thing: Duane was an egocentric sociopath who hadn't just gotten away with murder for thirty years; he'd gotten away with murder period. To break him, they had to get inside his head. For help with that, they contacted the FBI's Behavioral Science Unit.

In November 2005, Special Agent Nick Vanicelli of the FBI's Denver office reviewed the file and recommended the Criminal Profiling Unit assist. That December, Isaacson and Brandt had a phone consult with Quantico. They were given a list of investigatory loose ends to tie up and a 14-page document titled General Assessment Questions. Give it to people who were close to Duane, the FBI said, but not anyone who might warn him. Tell them to answer as if it was 1973.

The FBI's questionnaire began with Duane's socio-economic status and relationships with his siblings and parents. It moved to his appearance, habits, employment, education, and interests. Did he embrace a structured belief system that influenced his behavior? What made him angry?

Then, on a scale of one to five, respondents were asked to rate his personal characteristics— introvert vs. extrovert, self-centered vs. concerned for others, rigid vs. flexible, manipulative vs. straightforward. The questionnaire was given to Jean and Dick Brickell, Cherrie Otto, and me.

In May 2006, the cold case cops met in Vanicelli's office

for a final consult with two profilers from Quantico.

Interview Duane and his kids at the same time but do it separately, the FBI said. Don't give them a chance to warn the others. Approach Barbara, Duane's second wife, when she's alone.

Can we use a timeline? Isaacson asked. Don't show him anything that isn't 100 percent accurate because he'll turn any error in his favor, they warned.

Make sure each interviewer is able to respond to all comments. There can be absolutely no "blank looks" or feeble responses from these people.

What about the kids? Isaacson asked. Have grand jury subpoenas in hand and don't be afraid to use them.

Oh, one last thing about describing the mother's death: Don't use the words homicide, murder, or kill.

38. Memory Redux

There is no way by which the events of the world can be directly transmitted or recorded in our brains; they are experienced and constructed in a highly subjective way, which is different in every individual to begin with, and differently reinterpreted or re-experienced whenever they are recollected.... The wonder is that aberrations of a gross sort are relatively rare, and that, for the most part, our memories are solid and reliable.
—Oliver Sacks | *Speak, Memory*

Many deceptive persons believe that lying about memory is the safest route to take. Deception and an untruthful person's asserted "lack of memory" about actions, events, incidents, or behavior often go hand in hand.... Spontaneous and unsolicited assertions of "I don't remember" indicate the interviewee is attempting to wipe out, erase, and suppress certain pieces of information represented by "lack of memory" phrases.
—Wendell Rudacille | *Identifying Lies in Disguise*

After I retired, I started studying the mind and memory. For example, I signed something but couldn't recall even signing my own signature. I feel my memory is very fallible. My mind is getting weaker.
—Duane Frye | 2006

JACKIE: But that's the house that your mother was living in?

JAN: I could not say yes this is the house... I don't really think of this as my family home. Um, it certainly could be.

* * *

JAN: I... just out of curiosity... how accurate is anyone's memory from that long ago?

JACKIE: Well, you know, some people remember more than others.

JAN: Right, but how accurate would that memory be?

JACKIE: Well, obviously not as accurate as it would have been at that moment, that day.

JAN: For example... I have been telling the story of how I shot an antelope... for, you know, decades.

JACKIE: Right.

JAN: And the whole story about how it happened and... I have a vivid memory... of that event. Turns out I didn't shoot that antelope. My sister did.

JACKIE: Ah.

JAN: And I walked up to it because she couldn't deal with having shot this antelope, and so I was the one who walked up and saw the quivering body with the, you know, big brown eyes.

JACKIE: Oh.

JAN: But I did not shoot that animal. I still believe I did. I mean, it is so clear in my mind. So... in terms of having accurate memories, I don't think people really do. And if you're going to go back that far... I think it's a big stretch to think that anyone, especially a vivid memory like that... I think that's why I remember that is because it was [an] incredibly vivid memory. And it was wrong. Completely wrong.

—Jan Frye | Interview by Investigator Jackie Gee 2006

On September 10, 2006, five teams of detectives fanned out across the country to interview Duane and his four children. They wanted to catch them unawares, but when Isaacson and Brandt rang Duane's door in Florida, he was on the phone, apparently with his younger daughter Lynn. Lynn also called her sister Jan during Jan's interview, but Jan didn't answer the phone.

Jan refused to identify a photo of the house where Betty was living when she was killed. She said she didn't remember being there that morning— the last time she saw her mother alive—or taking her brother Greg to Doug's karate class in Boulder. Nor did she want to refresh her memory by looking at what she'd told the cops and the grand jury in 1973. Instead, she questioned whether anyone's memory is real. She did remember that Duane's arrest made her livid with anger. Now, when it became clear that he was the focus of the new investigation, she terminated the interview.

Humans are complex creatures with simple defenses: repress it, fight it, debate it, or kill it. We can simultaneously hold conflicting ideas, like self-justification and knowledge of guilt, but most of the time we dismiss what conflicts with our dominant viewpoint. Denial is a beautiful gift.

But wholesale rejection of the validity of memory— anyone's memory— ignores this fact: without it, we can't learn from experience. And if recall is selective, how do you look truth in the face and grapple with it?

39. Kill Your Darlings

In writing, you must kill all your darlings.
—**William Faulkner**

Q: How do you feel about the case being reopened? Do you think it's a good thing that… we're trying to solve your mother's death or do you think it's something that should be left alone?

A: I … you know, right off the top of my head, it's not something I'm really interested in doing. You know, I haven't given it much thought since it just happened. So, you know, it's not something—

Q: Can you tell me why you – um, what your reasons for not being interested in doing –is it for your mental health or—

A: You know, the family's pretty much come to grips with what we had to deal with with our mother's death. And going through it again doesn't seem like a fun idea. You know, it doesn't seem like it's going to be helpful to anybody.

* * *

Q: When you saw your dad that day, do you remember what type of clothing he was wearing?

A: Dark colored clothes. But that is about the best I can do.

Q: How about any injury? Physical injury?

A: He had a scrape or something. I remember he had a band-aid on his forehead. I believe. He had some sort of scrape.

Q: Is that something you brought to his attention and asked him about or what makes you remember that?

A: Because it was … as time went on, that was … anything that was unusual was burned into my brain. So that was kind of burned into my brain because that was unusual.

* * *

Q: Is there anything about the case that I haven't asked you about or you hadn't told the authorities at some point?

A: I really don't have any information about the case other than that my father was a suspect. And that was it. If there are other suspects I'd be interested because I never heard about it.

Q: Well, I think I can tell you that I don't think there are any other suspects. That the only suspect is your father. And right now the sheriff's office – it's believed that your father is responsible for your mother's death.

A: So somehow I see my dad getting arrested here?
—**Doug Frye | Interiew by Investigator Rick Sheets 2006**

In 1973, the grand jury summoned Doug twice. To every question, including our address, whether he taught karate, and if he resided in Boulder, he said I wish to speak to my attorney. He left the courtroom to confer with Duane's lawyer two dozen times. When he eventually did answer, it was only the most basic questions and in the same flat tempo, unapologetically telling the frustrated grand jurors that he was 19 years old.

In 2006, Doug was more open and forthright. He told the investigators he had bipolar disorder. Unlike his sister Jan, he remembered the day Betty was murdered, Duane's strange trip to Boulder, and the events surrounding his mother's death. He even sketched the layout of the laundry room and the passageway to the garage.

The interview was audiotaped. For much of it, Doug's cadence is robotic and halting. But at the end, when he asks about other suspects and if his dad will be arrested, he sounds interested. To my ear, he even sounds relieved.

The detectives asked Doug about a trip he'd taken to

Florida in 1981. Doug claimed it had nothing to do with the murder. In his third year of med school, he'd been in a suicidal depression and had gone to see Duane for help. But Duane told the investigators Doug wanted to talk about Betty's death.

In any case, Doug wasn't in Florida for long. He was a superb swimmer, but Duane was so afraid he'd commit suicide by jumping off a sea wall that after two days he flew Doug to Philadelphia and committed him to a psychiatric facility.

This is how I remember it.

Over Christmas break in 1980, we visited my folks in Brooklyn. Doug's sister Lynn lived near Philadelphia, and while we were back East, he told me he wanted to talk to her about Betty. This was the first time he'd said he wanted to talk to one of his siblings about his mother's death. He took the bus to Philly. When he returned, he was shattered. She couldn't believe I had doubts, he told me. She always knew Dad killed Mom.

Back in Colorado, Doug could barely drag himself to class. His med school advisor told him to take the quarter off. He started coming with me to my law school classes and began seeing a shrink. One snowy day, he went out jogging and swallowed every pill in our medicine cabinet. A motorist found him lying in a drainage ditch and brought him home. I put him in a hospital.

Doug swore he wouldn't harm himself again and was

released. Then he flew to Florida. The note I found on our kitchen table said he had to talk to his dad.

Duane called and said Barb had gotten a message that Doug was coming. Do I have to be there? he asked. For the next three days, radio silence—when I called Florida, there was no answer. Then my mom called. Doug had phoned her from Philly. Duane had flown him to a psychiatric clinic at the University of Pennsylvania and left him there. Could she give his shrinks my number?

That night, they called me. What can you tell us about Doug? they asked. We didn't even know he was married. The only thing Duane had told them was that Doug had some crazy fantasy Duane was involved in Betty's death.

Doug phoned me every night from the hospital—tortured, apologetic, drugged. He came home to an in-patient clinic in Boulder. Duane flew to Colorado. At the clinic, there was an altercation and Duane was told not to return. Who are they to tell me I can't see my son? he ranted. When Mom visited Doug, she saw something new in him—not just anger, but rage.

Slowly, Doug re-emerged. He finished med school, but nothing was the same. He was harder, cold. One day, he went hiking with a law school classmate of mine. They saw a baby bird that had fallen from its nest. Doug knelt beside it on the trail. He picked up a rock and bashed its brains out. An act of mercy, he said.

A writer's darlings are characters, plot lines, even phrases that you love most. You kill them because, like an unwanted son, they serve no purpose in your story.

40. Black Holes

black hole 1: a celestial object that has a gravitational field so strong that light cannot escape it and that is believed to be created, esp. in the collapse of a very massive star **2 a:** an empty space: VOID
—Merriam-Webster's Collegiate Dictionary, Eleventh Edition

I notice you're not coming to the family and saying would you like us to pursue this?
—Jan Frye | 2006

GRAND JUROR: Should the person who murdered your mother be punished?

A: Do I care if the person—do I want vengeance, or should the person who murdered my mother—

GRAND JUROR: Should the person who murdered your mother go to jail for murdering her?

A: Do I believe in justice, that somebody who murdered my mother should go to jail? I don't care.

GRAND JUROR: Why?

A: Because the fact that my mother is dead is all that's important to me. I don't care about revenge. To me, that

whole thing is revenge.... I don't know what happened, but would I be interested in putting my father in jail if there was evidence that my father did it? No, I wouldn't.
—Lynn Frye | Arapahoe County Grand Jury 2006

When investigators knocked on her front door in Florida, Lynn was at work. Her husband Jerry answered. Jerry had been a cop for 30 years. You're not opening that can of worms, are you? he said. We've always known he did it. This is going to wreck our lives.

The detectives interviewed Lynn at work. The day Betty was murdered, Lynn remembered Duane coming to Boulder to look at restaurants for Doug's wedding. She was busy hiding the fact that she was living with her boyfriend Don. Her mom believed all that Catholic bullshit, she said, that everyone who didn't have Catholic beliefs would go to hell, especially for having an abortion or cohabiting before marriage.

When they told Lynn that Duane had confessed to his mother Lolita, Lynn broke down. My mom's gone, she said. Now I'm going to lose my dad. My poor dad. She asked if Duane would go to jail in Colorado. When they said he would if he was convicted, she began crying again. Nobody even lives there anymore, she said.

They told her that her aunt Cherrie had come forward with the confession. That bitch, Lynn said. I hope she's happy.

41. Willful Blindness

Most people have a belief in the inner core of themselves as being good. So that whatever they've done, they'll say, "That's not the real me."
—**Theodore Dalrymple** | *Unraveling the Mystery of Murderous Minds*

We think well of ourselves because we are loved and we will fight fiercely to protect the key relationships on which our esteem depends. And that seems to be just as true even if our love is based on illusion.
—**Margaret Heffernan** | *Willful Blindness: Why We Ignore the Obvious at Our Peril*

According to former BBC reporter Margaret Heffernan, we blind ourselves to unpleasant truths because it makes us feel safe. Parent-child and marital relationships are particularly susceptible to illusions, and cementing a family's "group-think" ensures that dissenters become the enemy. Heffernan also points out that maintaining illusions insulates us from having to act on the knowledge we would otherwise acquire.

Even apart from politics, willful blindness and moral

non-accountability abound. From Rupert Murdoch's insistence that although he was "shocked, appalled, and ashamed" by the *News of the World* phone- hacking scandal, he personally was not to blame but was betrayed by unnamed "people I trusted"; to residents of multi-million-dollar homes built on a South Dakota floodplain who were wiped out by rising waters, but insist they'll rebuild (without insurance again, because floods like that only happen once a century); to the inhabitants of Uravan, Colorado, an abandoned uranium and vanadium mining-town- turned-Superfund site, who'd like nothing better than for the industry that destroyed their town and their loved ones' lives to start mining again.

One striking example is the 2009 Air France crash off the coast of Brazil, with all on board lost. The cause was a mystery until black boxes and cockpit voice recorders provided the answer: equipment failure compounded by pilot error. The plane's speed sensors had iced, disengaging the autopilot system.

The captain was asleep in the crew rest area and two co-pilots were at the controls. Neither was trained to fly in manual mode or respond to the malfunction. When the engines stalled and the plane began dropping, they did exactly the wrong thing: they pointed the nose up, which worsened the loss of forward momentum, instead of pointing the nose down, which would have enabled the plane to regain speed.

If the situation weren't so tragic, Air France's response

would be laughable. It lauded the crew, saying they showed an unfailing professional attitude and remained committed to their task to the very end. At this stage, the airline added, there was no reason to question the crew's technical skills.

Willful blindness has upsides. It allows us to preserve loving relationships, and families to exist. You can't get through the day without it; if you consciously focused on all the things you'd otherwise blind yourself to (Greenland melting, say, or the Amazon rainforest burning up), you'd become paralyzed. And supporting a uranium mine that's destroying your town is a matter of personal dignity if it lets you put food on the family table. But does it make you safe?

Betty Frye's blindness to the realities of her marriage may have cost her her life.

42. Footnotes

footnote: 1. An ancillary piece of information printed at the bottom of a page.
—*Oxford English Dictionary*

Of all Duane's children, the cold case cops thought Greg was the most likely to talk. Just 13 when Betty was murdered, he'd been with Duane when her body was found. Even if he had no first-hand knowledge of his dad's guilt, they believed he knew more than he'd said in 1973. But Greg was always an afterthought.

Days after Betty's murder, Duane had shipped Greg off to her family's farm in Kansas. They hoped farm work would keep his mind off her death. But Greg was a zombie. He spoke to no one, and a cousin had to do his chores. He returned to Colorado, and Duane called Betty's sister Lucene. Lu was Greg's godmother, but she didn't know him. She didn't even attend Greg's baptism; she'd participated by proxy over the phone.

Duane sent Greg to live with Lu in California. Greg was so out of it that Lu feared he was on drugs and took him for counselling to her parish priest. Greg eventually admitted to Lu that he'd seen Betty's body on the garage floor.

Greg lived with Lu nearly a year. He arrived after Betty's funeral in June and returned to Colorado in late November to testify at Duane's trial. When the charges against Duane were dismissed, Lu assumed he'd keep Greg for the holiday weekend. Duane didn't even keep that poor kid for Thanksgiving, she told her sister Jean. He sent him right back to us. Years later, Greg thanked Lu for saving his life. If it wasn't for you, he told her, I would never have made it. Now the cold case cops hoped Greg would open up to investigator Eric Smith.

Greg lived in a secluded enclave in the mountains of New Mexico. Smith told Greg and his wife they'd developed new information about his mother's death. Is there a new suspect? Greg asked. Smith said he couldn't give him any details. Greg said when the case was first investigated, his father went through hell and, if he was re-arrested, it would kill him.

Greg was hesitant to talk and kept conferring with his wife. It's vital we interview you as soon as possible, Smith told him. Greg dropped his head. I'll talk to you, he said. What do you need to know? Smith suggested it might be more comfortable at headquarters. Greg agreed to follow the detectives to Albuquerque in his own car. He promised not to contact family members on the way down, but said he'd likely be speaking to his wife on his cell phone.

At police headquarters, Smith offered Greg water. Greg was this close to talking, but suddenly he stopped. I want to talk to my lawyer, he said. Greg had completely shut down. Smith tried to convince him how important the interview was.

It seems unlikely you have a new suspect, Greg replied. My understanding is it was a random robbery. I'm resigned to the fact that the person responsible for my mother's death will never be found.

Smith gave Greg his cell number. The next day, as he was preparing to return to Denver, he called Greg one last time. Greg said he'd spoken to his lawyer and wasn't going to talk.

Years later, I made the trip to Greg's mountain myself.

Smith and Greg could have walked down Greg's dirt road and talked, or sat over a cup of coffee at the crossroads café. That solitary drive to Albuquerque, half an hour but a universe away, forced Greg from his refuge. It took him from his wife and kids on a Sunday afternoon and gave him time to think.

Why was he driving all that way, to a place he didn't want to go, to talk to cops about things he didn't even want to think about? The closer he got to Albuquerque, the less sense it must have made.

And all the way down, he was talking to his wife.

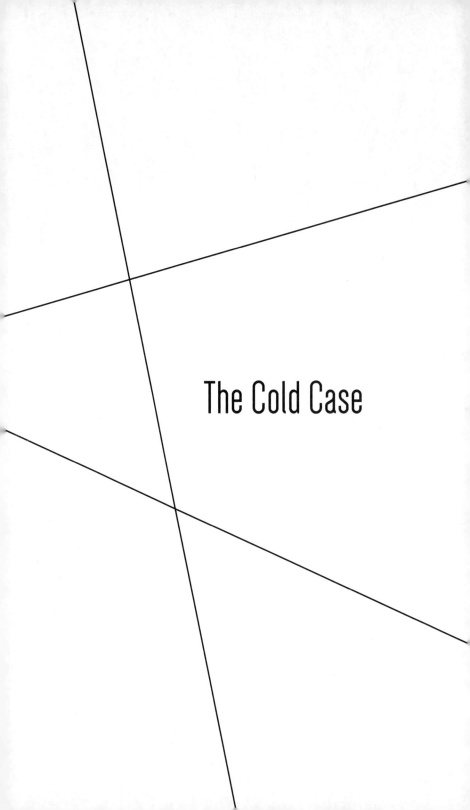

The Cold Case

43. Antagonists

antagonism/1 Mutual resistance of opposing forces; active opposition, a feeling of hostility or opposition.
—*The New Shorter Oxford English Dictionary*

---

antagonist/2: an agent of physiological antagonism: as a: muscle that contracts and limits the action of an agonist with which it is paired – called also antagonistic muscle.
—*Merriam-Webster's Collegiate Dictionary, Eleventh Edition*

One didn't want to lose and the other was lazy.
—**Bob Sendle | 2014**

Cops and DAs play on the same team. For the victim, against the perp—for justice. Sure, they play different roles. Cops investigate; DAs prosecute.

DAs have an ethical duty not to take a case to trial without probable cause. But probable cause is anything over 50/50, a far lower burden than the beyond-a-reasonable-doubt required to convict. Good DAs don't need a slam-dunk to take a case to trial.

Like pumping iron, opposition strengthens a case. DAs

and cops are also natural opponents. One pounds the pavement, the other a legal pad. Cops aren't perfect; they, too can rush to judgment. And sloppy police work can doom a case. Approach a witness clumsily or too aggressively and the witness shuts down. Miss a key question and you may not get a second chance. Forget to put it in your notes or report and you or the witness gets torn apart on the stand. But honest mistakes pale beside a DA's cynicism.

In 1973, Bob Sendle's antagonist wasn't Duane. It was the DA. When I sat down to talk with the twinkly-eyed prosecutor twenty years later, he threw Sendle under the bus all over again.

As Duane's trial advanced against a headwind of defense motions in 1973, the DA threw more and more ADAs at it. (One later became a judge; another was disbarred.) That fall, an ADA gave Duane's team the fingerprint charts of two kids who'd tried to burglarize a local burger joint called Georgia Boys. Those prints were supposed to be compared to prints defense investigator Jim Blake claimed he found at Duane's house. The ADA never got the second set of prints.

The morning Betty was killed, roofer Randy Peterson, who had a bird's-eye view of Duane's backyard, saw a man fiddling with the gate. Peterson described the man under oath. Until Blake massaged the description, he looked nothing like either Georgia boy. In fact, he looked like Duane. When the defense complained that Sendle didn't pursue an eyewitness (presumably the roofer), the DA obliged them by benching his lead cop.

Duane's alibi morphed into a timeline that defied the laws of physics. He couldn't explain away the kid who came to his door soon after Betty was killed, but he didn't need to. The DA did his work for him. On the eve of trial, the prosecution dropped the case based on unspecified "new information." Sendle took one for the team.

Forty years later, the old cop had a different take.

The DAs always wanted more, Sendle told me. Every time we went to them, they turned us down. If a person didn't plead guilty or give a written statement, they didn't want anything to do with it. One said he didn't want a failure. They dropped the case because it was easy for them.

History, it turns out, would repeat itself.

44. Just the Facts

FACT: A thing done; an action performed or an incident transpiring; an event or circumstance; an actual occurrence. An actual happening in time and space or an event mental or physical.
—Black's Law Dictionary, Revised Fourth Edition

INFERENCE: A process of reasoning by which a fact or proposition sought to be established is deduced as a logical consequence from other facts, or a state of facts, already proved or admitted.
—Black's Law Dictionary, Revised Fourth Edition

But facts are facts and flinch not.
—Robert Browning

Our justice system is based on facts. Not just that they exist, but that they can be known.

Cops deal with facts. DAs start there too; if they don't have enough facts, they tell the cops to get more. Facts become the basis for logical inferences. Persuasiveness—winning—depends on the prosecution's and defense's ability to weave inferences into competing narratives to tell juries.

Jurors are instructed that they can draw inferences from proven facts. They can't read a defendant's mind; without a confession, how else can they discern what went on in his head? Reasonable doubt is itself an inference: if the only inference beyond a reasonable doubt is guilt, the defendant is convicted.

But advocacy is more than logic. It takes courage and heart. If a DA can't wrap his head around the facts or fears he can't sell them to a jury, he dismisses the facts or refuses to draw inferences. And like a house of cards, the case falls apart. Don't think a jury of an engineer's peers can infer he beat his wife to death based on the crime scene and his behavior? Not so hard to tell yourself maybe he didn't do it.

But back to facts. The most unflinching advocate can only make an argument. Finding facts is the job of the judge and jury.

Perception bias is the human tendency to be partial, to make judgments based on our own way of looking at the world. Jury selection tries to ferret out biases. Judges are human too. Good ones put their biases on the table with every case over which they preside. Consciously setting biases aside makes it harder for them to sneak in later. But how do judges and juries decide a certain set of facts is true?

One thing they don't do is average out conflicting accounts or conjure up a blended version of reality. As in normal daily interactions, they weigh what they see and hear and run it through the lens of experience. This weeds out what neurologist Oliver Sacks referred to in the context of memory as (thankfully rare) "aberrations of a gross sort."

It frees jurors to come to a shared narrative truth, a shared sense of the event defined and refined by their role as finders of fact. Instead of creating fiction, they usually arrive at reliable verdicts. But verdicts are only as reliable as the facts presented by an advocate who actually believes them.

45. Telling Time

I have measured out my life with coffee spoons.
—**T.S. Eliot** | *The Love Song of J. Alfred Prufrock*

A pivotal factor in criminal cases is time.

Time of death can rule a suspect in or out. Minutes can make or break an alibi. Testimony is meaningless unless the witness can pinpoint precisely where he was and when.

But time is only as reliable as the means by which it's measured, and the clocks and watches in Betty Frye's time weren't as reliable as they are today. Indeed, there seems to have been a quaint tolerance of inaccurate timepieces.

The day Betty was killed, the watch on her wrist stopped at 10:03. She fell on that hand and the crystal cracked. Cops took the watch to a jeweler. Despite the damage, the watch was useless in pinpointing when she was attacked. It needed to be cleaned and lubricated, and blood running into the mechanism could have affected the time. The jeweler believed Betty's watch had been running intermittently—stopping and starting again—before she was killed.

Colorado State Patrol Officer Clyde Wiggins also wore a watch. That morning, he was handing out tickets at the busy intersection near the Fryes' home. According to his ticket book (i.e., his watch), Wiggins cited a VW at 10:20 and a motorcycle at 10:27. In 1973, Wiggins told investigators he was certain of the times of both stops. This was important not just because Wiggins was virtually on the scene when Betty was killed, but because other witnesses saw him and thought he was there an hour earlier.

Virginia Moldenhauer carpooled with Betty to work. Between 9:00 and 9:30 that morning, she dropped by the Frye house to return a thermos Betty had left in her car. She saw Wiggins ticket the VW and motorcycle. She was sure of the time because she planned to visit her son before he left for work at 10:00 a.m. Her daughter-in-law said she arrived at their house between 9:50 and 10:00.

The roofers on the house cater-corner to the Fryes had a clear view of the intersection. They, too, saw Wiggins ticket the VW and motorcycle. (Other than the killer, roofer Randy Peterson was probably the last person to see Betty alive, at 10:00 a.m. He also saw an unidentified male in the Frye backyard 15 or 20 minutes before the DJ on his radio announced the time at 11:30. These times tally with the cold case coroner's estimate of Betty's time of death, and Bret Wacker, who placed Duane at home at 11:35.)

But back to the testimony of Officer Wiggins. The roofers said Wiggins talked to one driver he ticketed for at least half an hour. If Virginia Moldenhauer arrived at the Frye house at the beginning of the traffic stops, and Wiggins gave one of the motorists grief for 30 minutes, it explains some of the discrepancy between her account of when Wiggins was there and the times in his ticket book. Investigators kept pressing Wiggins. Finally, he admitted his watch ran fast.

The most graphic and chilling evidence against Duane came from three electric clocks. The clocks stopped when the killer unplugged them from upstair bedrooms and the kitchen to stash in the loot by Betty's body in the garage. Photographed by investigators at the scene, they read 11:22, 11:23 and 11:27 a.m. Their GoPro-like documentary of the killer's minute-by-minute trek through the house was a cornerstone of the prosecution's case. But one fact isn't in the record.

In 2014, Bob Sendle told me a crime scene tech had plugged the clock-radio back in to play music. Did that affect the time? By a minute or two at most, Sendle said, and he thinks it happened after the clocks were photographed. But boy did he chew that tech out!

The most reliable indicator of time in Betty's case may have been a TV set. When Bret Wacker came to Duane's door at 11:35 a.m., he could prove the time. *The Monkees* ended at 11:30 and he'd switched the channel to *Sherlock Holmes* for his brother before his three-minute walk to Duane's house. Luckily, Bret didn't need a clock or a watch to back him up. He had *T.V. Guide*.

46. Moral Dimension of Time

And what rough beast, its hour come round at last,
Slouches toward Bethlehem to be born?
—W.B. Yeats

In 2005, the cold case cops faced a fight. Their true adversary was more formidable than Duane or any lawyer. A cold case is about time, and time is always on the defendant's side.

Time is the cop's enemy. The moment a crime is committed, the investigatory clock starts ticking. It's a truism that the first 24 or 36 hours are critical to solving a case. When a suspect is identified, time continues to favor the defense. In addition to statutes of limitation and strict filing deadlines, each passing day increases the risk of evidence being lost, witnesses dying, and memories failing. Time becomes the prosecutor's enemy.

In a cold case, these factors multiply a thousand-fold.

Time acquires a moral dimension, and its passage creates a new defense. Now the defense lawyer stands time on its head: Time itself—not his client—becomes the culprit and truth the victim. In robbing him of his right to a fair trial, the ticking clock is the cold case defendant's best friend.

The Family

47. Backstory

Backstory: The characters' lives before the story, novel, or film began.
—Sol Stein | *Stein on Writing*

Do nothing to shame your seven sisters
—Cundy Orten

Doug's favorite aunt was Betty's sister, Jean Brickell. The Thanksgiving after Betty was murdered, we went to Jean's house. That Christmas, Jean's mother Cundy visited from Kansas. Because Jean invited us but not Duane, Doug cut off all contact with her and his grandmother.

In 2008, Jean and I met briefly outside the Arapahoe County courtroom. We were sequestered and couldn't talk about the case. As Jean described Christmases with her family, and a special shrimp dish she always made, I imagined for an instant that she was Betty—that if she'd lived, we might one day have had the sort of relationship I never really had with my mom. We agreed to talk when the case was over.

In 2011, I called Jean. Jean said being married to Duane

changed Betty: Betty was afraid of him. Jean invited me over.

Jean still lived in the brick house in southeast Denver where we'd gone that long-ago Thanksgiving. Now in her mid-80s and widowed, she greeted me with a hug. She was as trim and elegant as ever in tailored slacks and a sweater set, her hair still short and red. Her stairwell was lined with photos of rawboned folks with tractors and pickup trucks on a wheat farm in Rawlins County, Kansas. Cundy had been born in a sod-covered dugout in the side of a hill. She and Charley Orten raised ten kids on that farm they bought at the height of the Depression.

Over frosted tea cakes in her den off the patio, Jean flipped through photo albums and reminisced about growing up. Cundy was a strict German Catholic. She mustered her daughters into brigades to cook, clean, and wash. None of you girls better get pregnant, she warned. Do nothing to shame your seven sisters. But Betty was special.

Jean turned to a photo of eight leggy gals vamping for the camera. Betty was the only blonde. With her blue eyes and curls, she looked like Shirley Temple. With that many sisters, Jean said, if you had anything outstanding, it was nice. No one could remember Betty driving a tractor or milking the cows. Her dad, Charley, bought her a player piano at an estate sale. Betty knew how to work him and Cundy too.

Jean smiled at the memory of dances at community halls. The rowdiest and best known was Tin Hall, built by Czech farmers in a neighboring parish. The Orten girls warned each other they better not marry a Bohunk (a Czech). Duane wasn't a Bohunk, but when Betty met him at a dance, Charley threw a fit.

Duane's father Herbert (Inky) Frye owned a tool shop in Atwood, Kansas, where Charley bought parts for his farm equipment. One day, Charley forgot his checkbook and, following a purchase, mailed Inky a check.

Next time Charley came to the shop, Inky insisted he owed him. Charley showed him the canceled check and Inky smarted off. That was the last time Charley set foot in Inky's shop. This fueled the antipathy between the families and set the stage for tensions in Betty's and Duane's marriage.

The Ortens were Catholic; the Fryes were Protestant. Inky and Lolita owned businesses in the county seat; the Ortens farmed. Cundy was proud of her German blood, but to Lolita, she and her daughters were Bohunks.

After Betty and Duane married, Lolita ridiculed everything Betty did, from the drapes she sewed to the crystal she chose. For the Ortens, Duane had nothing but contempt.

Betty gave birth to Jan and Lynn in rapid succession. When she got pregnant a third time, Duane didn't want another child. Betty miscarried and had a breakdown. Duane put her in Mount Airy, a Denver psych facility, where she received shock treatments. Right after Betty was released, she became pregnant with Doug. She was placed on lithium, but a breakdown always loomed. Duane blamed Cundy. It's your damn fault! he lashed out at her on a trip to Kansas. If she has another damn breakdown, how about if you pay for it?

In a few short years, the most special girl in Rawlins County had gone from a perfect wife whose life revolved around Duane, to a vulnerable woman who depended on him like a child. Worse, she kept saddling him with unwanted kids. At the Mexican restaurant the night before she was killed, she watched him laugh and drink with Barbara Dean. Jean thinks Betty confronted Duane about Barb that night or the next morning.

When the charges against Duane were dropped, Barb invited Jean to lunch. Everything is going just as we planned, Barb said. Duane and I are starting to date. The last straw was the following October, when Duane asked Jean to tell Cundy he and Barb were getting married and to represent Betty's family at the wedding. Jean refused.

Thirty-eight years later, night was falling through Jean's patio doors. She'd been talking for hours, but there was one thing more. Cundy and Betty talked right before she was killed, she told me. Cundy wasn't happy about Doug marrying you.

The abortion? I thought.

You're Jewish, Jean said.

48. Flashback

Flashback: A scene that precedes the time of the present story.
—Sol Stein | *Stein on Writing*

Ground zero 1: the point directly above, below, or at which a nuclear explosion occurs **2:** the center or origin of rapid, intense, or violent activity or change **3:** the very beginning: SQUARE ONE.
—*Merriam-Webster's Collegiate Dictionary, Eleventh Edition*

Childhood of D. – Sisters very close in age 16 months – sisters shared bedroom – D babysitting & female cousin staying at house – Duane had sex with cousin in bed with sisters & made them watch.
—Investigator Bruce Isaacson | Undated notes of interview of Cherrie Otto

---

I'm sorry I ever started it.
—Cherrie Otto, 2011

During the cold case, Duane's sister Cherrie sent me a message through DA Tomsic that she wanted to meet for lunch. We couldn't discuss our testimony. But at the deli, Cherrie was just as I'd remembered: pint-sized and delightfully improper, with a booming laugh and a whiskey voice. I'll tell you everything when it's over, she said.

In 2011, I tracked Cherrie down through her ex-husband Hank. After Betty was killed, Hank helped the neighbors clean the garage. He vividly recalled the blood. It was a mess, he said. We were cleaning till late that night. He told me Cherrie was in assisted living at The Verandas west of Denver. She's a lifelong smoker with congestive heart failure, he said, but she'll remember.

I called The Verandas. When Cherrie came to the phone, I sensed a new hesitancy in her voice. Her first words were, Duane's still alive, isn't he? The next day, I went to The Verandas.

Cherrie was frail but seemed her old self. Interviewing witnesses as a lawyer had taught me a hard lesson about taking notes: get the exact words. With Jean Brickell, I'd filled an entire legal pad. I hadn't wanted to break the flow by asking Jean if I could record the interview, but Cherrie readily agreed to being taped. We began with Atwood, Kansas, where she and Duane grew up.

The ugliest frickin' town you ever saw, Cherrie said—a snotty little burg in a valley one corner Swedish, one corner German, one corner Irish, and one corner Bohunk. She and her siblings worked at Frye Auto & Electric. Duane repaired radiators, Shirley built carburetors, and little Cherrie swept the floor. Shirley and I were Irish twins, she said with a wink. It was more like a year and a half apart, but we shared a bed.

Duane was named Herbert after his father, but neither of them went by that name. Inky Frye was an avid science fiction reader. He was hospitalized for depression at Mount Airy, the same psych facility where Betty later received shock treatments.

Duane and his mother Lolita were inseparable—two of a kind. Duane was ashamed that his father wasn't perfect, and Lolita was intolerant of Inky's problems. Duane never talked about Betty's issues as much as he talked about admiring her perfection; I guess it was a flaw in her perfection, Cherrie said. Duane was so ashamed of Betty's illness that he never told his children she was hospitalized or why.

Cherrie and Hank had been part of Duane's and Betty's upwardly mobile social set. That ended when Duane made Betty tell Cherrie they would no longer see them except on holidays. Hank was an engineer like Duane, but they just weren't on his level. Cherrie disliked Duane for other reasons. He didn't understand why their sister Shirley was so upset when her eldest son died. She had seven more kids, didn't she?

Cherrie had no problem talking about Atwood, her parents, or Duane as an adult. But when I asked what he was like as a boy, she was vague or changed the subject. In small towns, boys and girls grew up apart, she said.

Girls had dolls, and boys got their first BB guns at age five and went hunting. Did Duane have girlfriends? I asked. Oh my, yes—he liked cute little blondes....

There had to be a ground zero.

When I shared my frustration later with the cold case cops, they seemed amused. She didn't tell you about the time Duane had sex with a cousin and made her watch? Marv Brandt said. Duane was in junior high, which meant Cherrie was nine or ten. DA Tomsic and the cops believed the cousin was disabled and Duane may also have assaulted Cherrie or her sister or made them participate. Irish twins, she'd said with a wink. We shared a bed.

In 2006, when Cherrie was on the stand in the cold case, Duane's lawyer told her she'd been surreptitiously taped when she met with Jean and Dick Brickell at Piccolo's. Cherrie was a proud woman, and she felt betrayed.

How stupid I was to reopen her wound by pulling out a tape recorder! But Cherrie was a trouper. Under cross-examination, where it really counted, she never faltered.

49. A Perfect Family

They had one of the most wonderful marriages I have ever known and my father could never have done such a thing to anyone, let alone to the woman he loved so much. And I think that you people did him an injustice when you told me you would do everything to find the people who did it and then arrested the person who could least have ever done such a thing.
—**Jan Frye | Arapahoe County Grand Jury 1973**

The children selected for the family projection process are those conceived and born during stress in the mother's life; the first child, the oldest son or oldest daughter, an only child of either sex, one who is emotionally special to the mother, or one the mother believes to be special to the father.
—**Murray Bowen | *Family Therapy in Clinical Practice***

American psychiatrist Murray Bowen studied the family as an emotional unit and analyzed it in terms of systems theory. According to Bowen, the smallest stable relationship is the triangle. A triangle relieves stress by diffusing it to a third person or another interlocking triangle. It also creates anxiety because there's always an "odd man out." Being odd man out can trigger depression or physical illness. The fundamental family triangle is mother, father, and child.

All families have secrets. Doug didn't know his sister Jan had a baby while she was in high school. Interviewed by cold case cops in 2006, Jan was forthcoming about this and recalled it as a bonding time with Betty. But Duane sold their house and moved the family to Huntsville, Alabama—except for Doug, who stayed with his aunt Cherrie so he could keep swimming with his team, and Jan, who gave birth in an unwed mothers' home in Denver.

Betty didn't even tell her closest sister Jean.

When Jean and Dick Bickell made a surprise visit to Huntsville that Thanksgiving, the girls were very stand-offish. Jean thought Betty hit the roof when Jan got pregnant and demanded that Duane ask Martin Marietta for the transfer to Huntsville. But uprooting her family did not stabilize it or her place in it.

Jan and Duane were close. To him, she was "Jin-Jan," the only pet name I ever heard him use. If Jan's defense of Duane in 1973 is any indication, Betty never regained the inside position. When Barb Dean entered the picture, a new triangle formed. Betty was again the odd woman out.

But at the time of her murder, there were other things on her mind too. She told Virginia Moldenhauer she was worried about Doug's upcoming wedding to a girl of whom she disapproved (me), and Jan's relationship with Fred, a boyfriend Betty loathed. Fred lived west of Boulder in Sunshine Canyon. Jan had dropped out of CU, and as she told the cold case cops, her life back then was sex, drugs, and rock 'n' roll.

The immediate problem was that Jan had brought home a dog which destroyed part of Duane's fence. The dog had to be given away, but Betty didn't want Jan to give it to Fred because that would give Jan an excuse to see him. The night before the murder, Jan left her parents' house with Fred for a Chick Correa concert and Sunshine Canyon. No wonder Betty started crying.

The next morning Betty phoned our apartment. The call was awkward and brief. She wanted us to give a message to Jan that a car she planned to pick up from them in Littleton was still in the shop. But Jan had a phone too, and they also had Fred's number. Maybe Sunshine Canyon was a call Betty simply couldn't make.

50. Working the Problem

That her mother had just started working again, part-time, when this happened. That her mom was the disciplinarian; she was the "Catholic martyr." That her mother was the only Catholic in the family. That her mother believed everyone who didn't have Catholic beliefs would go to hell especially for having an abortion or cohabiting prior to marriage.
—**Investigator Liesl McArthur | Interview of Lynn Frye 2006**

[The deferring style of solving problems correlates] significantly to a lower sense of personal control, lower self-esteem, less active problem-solving skills, less tolerance for individual differences, and a greater sense of control by chance.... [Deferring] seems to be part of a passively-oriented lifestyle in which individuals rely on external structures and authority to deal with problems which they are less able to resolve.
—**Kenneth Pargament | *Religion and the Problem-Solving Process: Three Styles of Coping***

[T]he Catholic church holds that God converts a heterosexual relationship via the sacrament of Holy Matrimony into a divine, eternal union that cannot be dissolved by human action.... [D]issonance between the reality and expectations of sanctified family relationships may trigger feelings of spiritual failure, thereby exacerbating individual and relationship maladjustment.

—Annette Mahoney, Kenneth Pargament, et al. | *Religion and the Sanctification of Family Relationships*

We weren't all like Betty.

—Agnes Burke | 2008

Kenneth Pargament is an emeritus professor of psychology at Bowling Green State University. He has studied how religion affects how we solve problems and cope with stress. Pargament has identified three problem-solving styles: self-directed, in which we take responsibility for solving the problem; deferring, in which we defer the responsibility to God; and collaborative, in which the responsibility is actively shared.

Duane's and Betty's styles were diametric to each other. How they approached problems may shed light on why Betty became increasingly rigid in her beliefs, how trapped Duane felt, and why he was attracted to Barb Dean.

As an Ayn Rand devotee, an engineer, and an efficiency expert whose kids called him "Mr. Work the Problem,"

Duane was clearly a self-directed problem solver. So loath was he to rely on external assistance that he couldn't bring himself to trust his doctors ("I had a bypass which I didn't need") or Jim Blake, the private eye responsible for his case being dismissed in 1973. In 2006, Duane recalled Blake as some guy who had a silly theory about tree bark he found on Duane's rug.

Betty's style was at the opposite end of Pargament's spectrum. Raised by her devout Catholic mother Cundy, Betty believed her duty was to raise good Catholic kids. Betty's religiosity brought Cundy's approval. The elaborate Easter dresses and bonnets Betty made for Jan and Lynn, and the jaw-droppingly glamorous outfits she wore to church, also speak to her desire for social gain. But her orthodoxy had a price.

Marrying a Protestant-turned-atheist (Duane) required Betty to wed in a Denver chapel instead of a cathedral or a Kansas church. Duane, too, paid a price: he had to sacrifice his religious views for hers. After two daughters in three years, Betty conceived a third child he didn't want. She miscarried and had a breakdown. At the psych facility, visitors were warned not to bring Betty religious tracts. After she was released, she promptly became pregnant with Doug. After she conceived Greg, Duane got a vasectomy.

Whatever competence Betty had going into her marriage was relentlessly undermined by Duane (These are my guests. You will treat them right!) and his mother Lolita (What hideous drapes!). He agreed to raise their kids Catholic but was dismissive of her religion (he could be so hateful about meat on Fridays, Jean said) and picked fights about it with Dick Brickell.

And Betty was failing in her duty to raise good Catholic kids. Eldest daughter Jan got pregnant out of wedlock. Golden boy Doug renounced religion and refused to attend church. Unbeknownst to Betty, Lynn was cohabitating with her boyfriend in Boulder.

As Betty turned increasingly to religion to cope, her world shrank. She couldn't turn to anyone for help—not even her closest sister, Jean.

The night before she was killed, she dealt with her problems by launching into a crying jag. According to Duane's confession, when she started crying again the next morning, it was the last straw.

Barb Dean was no fashion plate, but she was president of the University of Illinois Accountancy Club. While Betty's world was crumbling, Barb could sit in a booth in a Mexican restaurant with Duane on a Friday night, have a drink, and laugh. When was the last time he and Betty had laughed?

Betty's belief that marriage was sacred put divorce off the table. Her duty was to give birth to and raise good Catholics. Duane's was to be bound to her in sickness and in health. With Doug and me at The Red Lion Inn after her murder, his resentment at his lost opportunities gushed out.

The day I testified in the cold case, Betty's sisters Agnes and Thelma were in the front row. When I left the witness stand, Ag hugged me and whispered in my ear. We weren't all like Betty, she said.

51. Embedded Narratives

Mise en abyme: In Western art history, a formal technique of placing a copy of an image within itself, often in a way that suggests an infinitely recurring sequence. In film and literary theory, it refers to the technique of inserting a story within a story. The term is derived from heraldry and literally means "placed into abyss."
—*Wikipedia*

An embedded narrative is a story within a story.

A single narrator tells a series of interlocking tales, like Scheherazade in *Arabian Nights*. A group of pilgrims recount their journeys to Canterbury in Chaucer's *Canterbury Tales*. Shakespeare's *Hamlet* has a play within a play.

Stories can be nested or interlocked, with flashbacks, dream sequences, or letters illuminating the main or framing story. Mary Shelley's *Frankenstein* opens with Captain Robert Walton writing to his sister about rescuing Victor Frankenstein on a voyage to the North Pole. This becomes the frame for Victor to recount his creation and pursuit of his humanoid monster, who in turn implores Victor to create a mate for him, and so on.

The visual arts are rife with infinite sequences. They appear in Russian nesting dolls. The original Quaker Oats man holds a box of Quaker Oats with himself depicted on it. The French have an evocative term for this type of hell—mis en abyme, which is translated as "thrown" or "cast" into the abyss.

But embedded narratives also have a meaning beyond their application to literature and art. They are interwoven systems by which we make sense of life.

Theology, nature, culture, law, society, and family all interconnect. A family's view of abortion is affected by its religion and culture. Betty and Duane's social system was defined by Martin Marietta's hierarchy and mores and the Arapahoe County subdivision where they lived. 1973 was also a time of cultural upheaval and assaults on authority.

Vietnam, antiwar protests, and the Pentagon papers. Vatican II tossing out Latin mass and meatless Fridays. Women's lib, *Roe vs. Wade*, birth control, and Betty Friedan's *Feminine Mystique*. A sexual revolution was going on right under Betty's nose. And Duane had left Martin while she went back to work to pay college tuitions and procure life insurance. The systems that made sense were coming undone. The narrative no longer held.

52. Emotional Shock Waves

The "Emotional Shock Wave" is a network of underground "after-shocks" of serious life events that can occur anywhere in the extended family system in the months or years following serious emotional events in a family. It occurs most often after the death or threatened death of a significant family member. It operates on an underground network of emotional dependence of family members on each other…. The nature of the human phenomenon is such that [a family] reacts vigorously to any such implications of the dependence of one life on another.

In my work with families, I carefully use direct words, such as death, die, and bury, and I carefully avoid the use of less direct words, such as passed on, deceased, and expired…. The use of direct words helps to open a closed emotional system.

—Murray Bowen | *Family Therapy in Clinical Practice*

When interview[ing] the children of [Duane] Frye, do not use the words "kill," "murder," or "homicide" to describe the death of their mother.

—Investigator Bruce Isaacson | Progress Report re FBI Behavioral Profiling Unit 2006

We lost Betty over the weekend. She ran head-on into
burglars.

—Duane Frye | 1973

Murray Bowen studied how emotional shock waves
affect a family's equilibrium. Any loss or addition to a
family disturbs its equilibrium, and the intensity of the
reaction depends partly on the functional significance of
the member who is added or lost.

As physical losses, Bowen cites a kid going off to college
or an adult child marrying and leaving home. Functional
losses include a key family member becoming
incapacitated by illness or injury which prevents him or
her from doing the work on which the family depends.
The physical and functional loss of a parent creates a
shock wave. Betty's murder produced a tsunami.

Even before the murder, several events upset the Frye
family's equilibrium. Doug left home twice: to go to
college and to marry me. Duane left Martin Marietta, a
decision that required Betty to shoulder the economic
responsibility for the family. Betty's significance to her
kids on all levels made her death a catastrophic loss.

When emotional dependence on the person who died is
denied, grief and mourning are cut off and the shock
wave goes underground. Symptoms run the physical
gamut (from colds and first signs of chronic illness, to
acute medical conditions) to the full emotional spectrum

(mild depression to phobias and psychosis). Not long after the murder, Duane suffered a multi-organ physical breakdown. Doug's mental breakdown followed.

In treating families after a member's death, Bowen described what happened with direct words. He also advocated having the most personal funeral service possible. The night before Betty's funeral in Kansas, Duane met with the priest. The priest didn't speak to Betty's relatives. At the funeral mass, the most personal thing he said about Betty was that despite her many problems, she always managed to be kind.

In 1973, Duane's children were required to attend his bail hearing as a show of support. When the DA sought to demonstrate the brutality of her murder by offering crime scene photos, Duane's lawyer, to demonstrate outrage, made us leave the courtroom. We were props. Duane's imposed cone of silence controlled what we were told and deprived his kids of any tangible association with Betty's death. It made her murder less real and set the stage for what followed.

When I saw Duane at The Red Lion Inn, his wedding band was gone. With it went any discussion of what really happened in the garage. The shock wave traveled underground for decades until the cold case drove it to the surface.

The Courtroom

53. Telling Details

telling: carrying great weight and producing a marked effect: EFFECTIVE, EXPRESSIVE.
—Merriam-Webster's Collegiate Dictionary, Eleventh Edition

The truth of the story lies in the details.
—Paul Auster | *The Brooklyn Follies*

A telling detail captures the essence of what is being described. Like a perfectly framed snapshot, it says more than it depicts. And it embeds itself in one's memory.

In May 2011, after the case was over, I had lunch with cold case cops Isaacson and Brandt at The Avalanche Bar & Grill, near the Arapahoe County Sheriff's Office, in a sports complex overlooking the rink where the Colorado Avalanche hockey team practices. I wanted to know what went wrong in 1973 and what the case had meant to them personally. Isaacson and Brandt immediately brought up their interview of Duane in Florida in 2006. They were struck by two details.

For Isaacson, it was the look on Barbara Frye's face and

what she did when they came to her door and identified themselves as Arapahoe County cold case cops investigating Betty's murder. Barb clapped her hands in excitement and said, You finally found who did it!

Brandt was struck by the way Duane looked at you. He sizes you up, Brandt said, trying to figure out if you're smart or Barney Fife or something. Apparently concluding they were Barney Fife, Duane led them from his front hall past a living room and kitchen whose counter opened onto a dining area. While the Florida cop stayed in the kitchen with Barb, Duane sat the cold case cops at the dining room table. He positioned himself at the end of the table facing the kitchen counter. The interview lasted an hour and a half. During the entire time, Duane watched Barb.

In 1982, I received a Hallmark card. The Christmas after Doug left, Barb sent it with a little note. I'm so sorry how things worked out, she said. Barb was the only member of the Frye family I ever heard from after our divorce.

54. The Crucible: Hydraulic Pressure of a Case

Crucible: In fiction, a situation or locale that holds characters together as their conflict heats up. Their motivation to continue opposing each other is greater than their motivation or ability to escape.
—**Sol Stein** | *Stein on Writing*

---

hydraulic pressure 3: operated by the resistance offered or the pressure transmitted when a quantity of liquid (as water or oil) is forced through a comparatively small orifice or through a tube.
—*Merriam-Webster's Collegiate Dictionary, Eleventh Edition*

A cold case is a crucible. The gnawing need for answers locks you in; the colder the case, the hotter the crucible becomes. The only escape is your day in court.

Court cases exert a hydraulic force. If you're swept up in one, you don't control it; it controls you. Add the chaos on which criminal defense lawyers thrive, and the courtroom becomes its own super-heated crucible.

Pressure leads to rationalizations, and misstatements lead to lies. The assignment of a new judge to the case provides a new apple to bite, a fresh opportunity to reargue what had been lost before. The crucible becomes unmoored from objective reality. But even chaos needs a narrative.

Like writers, lawyers seize a fact and run with it to create a narrative on which to build a case. Duane's defense was simple: his elderly sister Cherrie and I had fabricated his confession in order to sell books. His lawyers subpoenaed *Quiet Time*'s twenty-odd drafts and my notes under the theory that each was a statement of fact they could use to impeach me with at trial.

To run out the clock on aging witnesses, the defense dragged out the pretrial hearing for eighteen months. Then the case traveled up and down Colorado's appellate courts. In the end, a different sort of justice would prevail.

55. Swatting Wasps

In January 2007, Duane was rearrested for Betty's murder. His daughter Jan posted his $100,000 bond. Though notified the previous September that he was the target of a grand jury investigation, he didn't cancel a planned trip with Barb to South America. But he did hire a lawyer.

Brooklyn has Court Street lawyers. Named for an area blocks from where I grew up, close to bail bondsmen and the courts, Court Street lawyers are streetwise. They are flashy dressers. Smooth talkers, hard-working and smart. Hustlers. If you are in trouble, they are the kind of lawyer you want with you in court. Gary Lozow may have been from Gary, Indiana, but he is a Court Street lawyer.

Tall and heavily built, Lozow wore mod glasses and Italian suits and slicked back his longish gray hair. He liked junk food and snacks, was quick with a self-deprecating joke, and was an even worse driver than me. He was charmingly disarming, and quick to forgive blunders. I knew these things about him, and more, because I knew Lozow. In 1992, he'd hired me to work at his criminal defense firm. We had the Jewish thing going, and we'd been more than colleagues. We'd been friends.

If four decades of practice had taught Lozow anything, it was to come out swinging. If Plan A was to defend on the basis of innocence, and Plan B to attack the prosecution, he chose B. Cops were never just negligent or made mistakes; it was either a conspiracy or bad faith. He settled on his narrative early and dug in his heels. If he couldn't bully or bluff a DA into dropping an indictment, he wore him or her down. When he lost a motion, he filed it again. When all else failed, he tried to run out the clock.

Lozow operated by a few inviolate rules. He didn't take a case until the money, Mr. Green, hit the table. He never asked a client for his story until after he showed him what the DA had. Like most defense lawyers, he didn't like putting clients on the stand. If they did testify, they were told not to overreach and to keep a cool head if confronted with statements they'd supposedly made. Statements were seldom recorded; instead, they were memorialized in investigatory reports or FBI 302s. How was the client to know if the cop got what he said wrong?

Lozow told me he liked defense work because it was easier to counter-punch than to punch. But for him, it was more than that, and I'd gotten a glimpse of the "more" more than once. That first spring, we conducted witness interviews together—sorority girls in a date rape case in Boulder. We met with them at the old law school one sultry afternoon. Tall windows were open to catch the breeze, and in flew a wasp. High above us, it lazily circled the table.

Lozow pretended to ignore it. Suddenly, he clambered onto the table and frantically began swatting at the wasp with his legal pad until he killed it. Then he calmly resumed his questioning.

At first, criminal defense work felt natural. My relatives had fled pogroms and distrusted the police. I'd written law review articles on the waiver of Miranda rights and the duty not to turn over incriminating evidence. And the courtroom was unexpectedly exhilarating. There was no time to second-guess or browbeat yourself; it was light years from structuring loans and advising banks on the Glass-Steagall Act at the Seventeenth Street firm where I'd gone to pay the mortgage after Doug walked out on me.

Ultimately, however, I wasn't cut out for the work. My problem was basic: I wanted to know the whole story. I wanted to catch witnesses in truths, not lies—to identify the common threads in their accounts. The novelist in me insisted on knowing *why*. And though I liked most of our clients, I didn't identify with them. Not the way Lozow did.

After we stopped working together, we stayed friends. When John and I married in 1993, Lozow was one of our huppah holders. When *Quiet Time* was published in 2001, he came to its launch. One Sunday in late 2006, he called us at home and asked to come over.

Duane had been referred to him by a business associate of his in Florida. It's always fun to handle a matter where you know the people involved, Lozow said, and would you mind if I take the case? We told him Duane had the right to choose his lawyer, and Lozow had the right to choose his clients.

Lozow didn't tell us he'd been following the grand jury proceedings and had asked DA Ann Tomsic not to call me as a witness. Tomsic had refused his request, and told him if our friendship posed a conflict, he shouldn't take the case.

Nor did we know he'd offered to plead Duane guilty in exchange for no jail time. Tomsic rejected that offer, too, because she didn't believe Duane would even admit Betty was dead.

In January 2007, I voluntarily sat down with Lozow's partner and paralegal and told them all I knew about the case.

A Brooklyn-born Jew was about to become Lozow's wasp.

56. Is That All There Is?

If that's all there is my friends, then let's keep dancing.
Let's break out the booze and have a ball...
—**Peggy Lee** | *Is That All There Is?*

Over the next two years, Lozow filed dozens of motions to dismiss the prosecution's murder charge. The passage of time denied Duane a fair trial, the DA was negligent and acted in bad faith, and anyone who said anything against Duane was lying. In one motion, he quoted Peggy Lee's *Is That All There Is?*

During the eighteen-month pretrial hearing, Lozow put the 1973 investigators and the cold case cops on trial. He resurrected Tom Gussie as Betty's real killer and Jim Blake as the dogged detective who'd broken the case. He attacked Duane's deceased mother, Lolita. He even used poor old Jim Dean, who'd died broken-hearted after wife Barb left him for Duane.

Although Jim had told Dick Brickell he wanted to get a gun and kill Duane, Lozow now claimed Duane's inability to call Jim as a witness was fatally prejudicial because Jim "could have provided important information about the Dean marriage at the time of [Betty's] death, and likely dispel the allegations regarding a suggested motive for [Duane murdering his wife]."

This time around, the DA's office was better prepared. To re-prosecute Duane three decades after the fact, they needed to show new evidence had been discovered in the interim. That put Cherrie and me in Lozow's cross-hairs. Seventy-eight-year-old Cherrie became Duane's "estranged sister" whose "cryptic assertion" related a "confession" or "story" that was "a figment of her imagination."

I was Doug's "former fiancée" who didn't know Duane because we'd met only a couple of times, and who had initiated the cold case in cahoots with Cherrie in order to sell books.

The DA's smoking gun was Duane's confession to Lolita. Because Cherrie had brought the confession to the cops, Lozow had to kill the messenger. It didn't matter if that meant establishing Cherrie's memory as faulty or that she'd misinterpreted what her mother said; that Lolita had been untruthful or of unsound mind, or that Cherrie herself was an out-and-out liar. In June 2007, when Cherrie took the stand, Lozow got more than he bargained for.

As Cherrie marched past the defense table, she saw Lozow turn to his young associate. The Kanes (John and me) are friends, he said just loudly enough for Cherrie to hear. We go to dinner together. Cherrie looked in vain for Jean Brickell. She knew Jean and her sisters had attended every pretrial hearing even if they had to wait in the hall. But today Jean hadn't come.

Suddenly, Cherrie felt completely alone. When she'd learned about the confession, she confided it to her best friend, Bette Smaldone, the assistant minister at her church, and a second friend she refused to name. Bette had confirmed the confession to the cold case cops, but now she, too, was dead. All Cherrie could think was, thank god Bette died before she had to run this gauntlet.

Cherrie's weakness was her inability to pinpoint the exact dates Lolita had told her about Duane's confession. On tape at Piccolo's, she'd said their conversations occurred in 1995 or 1996. She'd also roughly estimated it as 25 years after Betty's murder which, if taken literally, was around the time Lolita went into a nursing home. With Cherrie on the stand, Lozow tried to push the date to 2001 or 2002, after Lolita developed dementia.

But Cherrie insisted that when Lolita recounted the confession, she'd been lucid and alert. Cherrie also testified that when saw me interviewed on a local PBS station about *Quiet Time,* she went out and bought my novel. After reading it, she called Jean Brickell.

Cherrie sidestepped Lozow's traps. Failing to confuse her on dates, exact words said, and whether her minister advised her to go to the cops in the 1990s, Lozow tried to get her to conflate the confession with *Quiet Time.* When he asked if Betty crying over my impending marriage to Doug was in the book, Cherrie demurred. I read two books a week, she said. Do you remember all your books? No, Lozow snapped, and I don't read two books a week.

Finally, Lozow threw it in her face that when she'd met with Jean and Dick Brickell at Piccolo's, they'd been wearing a wire. Cherrie hadn't known. On the stand, she kept her cool, but she never forgave Jean. And her dignity wasn't all she lost.

Outside the courtroom, Cherrie made an overture to her niece Jan. Infuriated, Jan rebuffed her. If you think I'm going to stand here making small talk with you, you're crazy, Jan said. One phone call to my father and none of us would be here. We could've cleared up this whole thing without a trial!

That was Cherrie's last contact with the Fryes.

57. Courtroom as Kabuki

kabuki: a form of traditional Japanese drama with highly stylized song, mime, and dance, now performed only by male actors, using exaggerated gestures and body movements to express emotions, and including historical plays, domestic dramas, and dance pieces.
—*dictionary.com*

In February 2008, I testified. Lozow had his former partner, Rick Kornfeld, cross-examine me.

Days earlier, the defense had subpoenaed the fragmentary reports former DA Gallagher had given me and the court file I'd obtained in 1994. Along with my thank-you note to Gallagher, the court receipt for the copying charges, and the date-stamped manila envelope in which the clerk had mailed me the file, I gave them to my lawyer, Hal Haddon.

Haddon specialized in white-collar criminal defense. Although both lawyers' clients ran afoul of the law, he and Lozow danced to very different tunes. Lozow sported hand-tailored Armani suits; Haddon's clothes didn't talk. Lozow mangled English and took pride in how few books he read; Haddon had represented Hunter S. Thompson. Lozow went for the gut; Haddon preferred the jugular. Lozow played his cases to the media. Haddon had one rule: Don't.

DA Tomsic wanted me to describe Duane's behavior the day of the murder and later at The Red Lion Inn. Kornfeld's job was to show this wasn't new evidence, either because I'd had a duty to come forward in 1973 or because the cops should have interviewed me back then. But when Haddon delivered the subpoenaed documents to Kornfeld just before Judge Valeria Spencer took the bench, an outraged Kornfeld accused me of grand jury abuse and demanded Spencer strike me as a witness or dismiss the case.

Tomsic pointed out that Duane's own lawyers had made the 1973 grand jury transcripts public by attaching them to motions in the court file—corroborated by the clerk's own envelope and receipt. Suddenly, Kornfeld's credibility was at stake, not mine. Like Wile E. Coyote at the edge of a cliff, he frantically backpedaled. But I was rattled. When I took the stand, Lozow was scribbling and passing notes to Kornfeld. And Duane was with them at the defense table.

The last time I'd seen Duane in a courtroom had been thirty-five years earlier, at his bail hearing. Manacled and in an orange jumpsuit that swallowed him, back then he'd looked scared. Facing him now was different than I'd imagined. As his icy eyes impaled mine, I felt an unexpected jolt of familiarity. He was angry—in control. Steps from the witness stand, in the first row of the gallery, Betty's octogenarian sisters Agnes and Thelma sat with their faces turned trustingly towards mine. I kept my eyes on Tomsic.

Tomsic walked me through the day Betty was murdered. Why didn't I talk to the cops in 1973? Because I was about to become part of Doug's family, I said, and they never asked.

Tomsic asked about Barb. Duane had been planning a cruise with Betty, I said. When Betty was killed, he'd wanted to take Barb instead, but the friends he was going with didn't approve....

Liar! Duane shouted.

Duane was half out of his chair, and Tomsic stood open-mouthed at the podium. Judge Spencer broke the silence. I will not stand for that, Mr. Frye! she said. Lozow told Judge Spencer that Duane was hearing-impaired and he'd tell him to whisper to himself, but she wasn't fooled. She warned Duane not to do it again. I looked squarely at him. Coldly, he returned my gaze.

A week after I testified, Judge Spencer ruled Cherrie and I had presented credible new evidence that justified reopening the case. Lozow's epic motion to dismiss the charges was denied.

We all knew who the real liar was.

58. Fact vs. Fiction

This investigator then inquired what *Quiet Time* meant and Lynn went on to explain: That *"Quiet Time"* was something that her mother had every afternoon with the kids. That during a two-hour time period, between 1:00 PM and 3:00 PM over the summer vacation, the kids were to be in the house, were not allowed to go outside, were not allowed to watch television [and] could play games quietly or read books while her mother slept for those two hours.

—Investigator Liesl McArthur | Interview of Lynn Frye 2006

Writers of fiction know that the best source of a good, believable story line and character information is from their own experiences in life, used in combination with real events. The writer takes these experiences and weaves them into a novel, while describing character traits of persons he has known. Relying on memories of things he knows happened, the writer then changes those memories while making up a story about things *that did not happen*…. It is important for a person who is making up a story about events and circumstances that never happened and characters that never existed to extract, convert, and apply some information obtained from real past experiences to try to make the story believable.

—Wendell C. Rudacille | *Identifying Lies in Disguise*

Although all literature in some sense derives from personal experience, it would be a serious misreading to assume that characters in a work of fiction are in any way "real." Characters in works of fiction, though sometimes inspired by actual people, are in fact combinations of the appearance, traits, and idiosyncrasies of many people, known and unknown to the author, and thus completely imagined and apart from reality.... Fictional truth has little or nothing to do with the "facts" of any real life event.

—Professor David Milofsky | Affidavit 2008

For Lozow, running out the clock paid off.

Duane's trial was set for September 2008. By then, the Arapahoe County court system had rotated Judge Spencer off the case. It was reassigned to Judge Charles Pratt, who'd been appointed to the bench three years earlier after being in a private civil practice.

Inheriting Spencer's courtroom on the eve of Duane's trial, Pratt was thrown into the case cold. Because the pretrial hearing had dragged on so long, DA Tomsic also had to withdraw to handle a death penalty case. The new prosecutor, Ryan Brackley, a veteran of the Manhattan DA's Office, had just moved out west, and would take her place.

Now the only side with institutional memory was the defense. How could Pratt and Brackley know every objection argued and won, or how witnesses had performed at the grand jury or in open court? Cold transcripts are a poor substitute for observing demeanor and how people held up under cross-examination. Motions for reconsideration had offered Lozow a perpetual second bite. Now Pratt was a whole new apple, and into his lap *Quiet Time*'s fate was dumped.

To Lozow, my mystery novel wasn't fiction. Instead, *Quiet Time,* my notes, and each of its 20-odd drafts were separate factual statements about Betty's murder that he could use to impeach my credibility. He subpoenaed everything.

Haddon moved to quash Lozow's subpoena. He argued *Quiet Time* was fiction, the subpoena was a fishing expedition into the creative processes of a novelist, and my notes and drafts were trade secrets and protected by the First Amendment. To educate Pratt on how novels were written, Haddon turned to David Milofsky, a prize-winning author and Professor of English at Colorado State University. Pratt accepted Milofsky as an expert in his field.

At the July 2008 hearing on our motion to quash, Haddon began by establishing that characters in a novel are often based on people the novelist knows. Novels don't live in a vacuum, Milofsky explained; writers are affected by everything around us, and by reordering events, we try to make sense out of life. Just because writing a novel requires imagination doesn't mean the novelist can't tell the difference between fiction and fact.

On cross, Lozow asked Milofsky if novels have non-fictitious characters. All characters in a work of fiction are fictitious, Milofsky said. How, Lozow asked, without knowing all the facts of the Frye case, could Milofsky opine that *Quiet Time* was a work of fiction? Milofsky analogized it to *War and Peace* (which Lozow said he'd read "I think 100 years ago"); it was based on France's invasion of Russia in 1814, but the characters were of Tolstoy's own creation.

Could you call *Quiet Time* a creative non-fiction novel? Lozow asked. No, I will call it a novel, Milofsky insisted.

Lozow then argued I wasn't a writer, but an advocate who'd inserted myself into the case. If you've written a book and gotten it published, are you forever a novelist? he demanded.

It tends to infect you, Milofsky replied. So you call it a disease, Lozow said. With that, he rested.

Pratt agreed *Quiet Time* was fiction but ordered the first draft to be produced in chambers. After privately reviewing it, he ruled my novel and everything else Lozow had subpoenaed was inadmissible.

59. Red Herring: The Strange Case of Vernon Maurice Roe

red herring/2 Something intended to divert attention from a more serious question or matter; a misleading clue, a distraction. Orig. in draw a red herring across the track, etc. (from the practice of using the scent of a smoked herring to train hounds to follow a trail).
—*The New Shorter Oxford English Dictionary*

Tom Gussie wasn't the only red herring Lozow dragged across the track to defend Duane. He also tried to pin Betty's murder on the killer in the unsolved death of Vernon Maurice Roe. Based on cold case websites and news articles at the time, here are the facts.

Roe was a 44-year-old Martin Marietta engineer who lived less than a mile from the Fryes. Recently separated from his wife in California, he'd attended a company Christmas party on Sunday, December 15, 1974.

He left the party early to tend to his dog before going to dinner with a co-worker. When Roe didn't show up for dinner, his date called him repeatedly but got no answer.

When he didn't come to work the next morning, she

went to his house. Roe's door was unlocked. She found him on his kitchen floor, shot three times in the chest. There was no sign of forced entry or struggle, and burglary was ruled out. On the Arapahoe County cold case webpage, Roe's case is still listed as UNSOLVED.

DA Tomsic recalled cigarette butts found at the crime scene. A neighborhood kid also remembered seeing a car with California plates parked near Roe's house the day he was killed. These facts suggest an execution or contract killing, perhaps related to Roe's pending divorce. Roe's case has certain similarities to Betty's murder: the victims were close in age, lived less than a mile apart, worked at Martin, and were killed at home on a weekend with burglary ruled out. But the dissimilarities are equally striking.

Roe was separated from his wife and living alone; he was killed in late afternoon or early evening; he was shot in his kitchen, and Betty was bludgeoned in her garage; there was no indication his crime scene was staged. The neighborhood was an enclave of people who worked at Martin Marietta. If the killer were stalking Martin employees in Arapahoe County, there was no shortage of targets, and why wait 18 months?

So why did one of the original cops in Betty's case believe the two murders were related? The answer may lie on the 2008 version of Arapahoe County's cold case webpage. The case after Roe's was Betty's (listed as SOLVED). Of greater interest is the case right before Betty's. Thanks to sharp police work, the murder of

Nadine Franklin was also SOLVED.

Nadine was a 15-year-old who ran away from a group home. Shot four times with .38 caliber bullets, she was found on a busy Littleton corner at 8:45 a.m. on December 31, 1971. As ACSO began to investigate, the Littleton PD received a shots-fired call at 11 a.m. near a shelter at a local park.

When cops arrived, they found a young man dead from a self-inflicted shot to the chest. A Smith and Wesson revolver lay next to the body and .38 cartridges were recovered. The young man had a history of mental illness and had been diagnosed with chronic paranoid schizophrenia. Littleton PD closed his case as a suicide.

An alert ACSO investigator thought Nadine's murder might be connected to the suicide. Bullets from both scenes were sent to the CBI, which found the same gun had been used.

Nadine was murdered 18 months before Betty, and almost exactly three years before Roe. What's the chance of an Arapahoe County cop in the 1970's not being aware of the clever police work that went into linking Nadine's murder with her killer's suicide and the kudos the investigator undoubtedly received? The ACSO still crows about it.

And in the aftermath of Duane's case being dismissed in 1973 and him being re-charged decades later (two black eyes for Arapahoe County), why not ruminate (or grumble) that instead of Duane having gotten away with murder, the Martin Marietta stalker had struck again?

Some defense lawyers throw spaghetti at a wall. Others draw stinky herrings across the track.

Shooting
the Survivors

60. Judicial Chutes and Ladders

Chutes and Ladders is a board game for kids. The board is illustrated with playground equipment, but the game itself is a luck-based morality play: land on a good square and scramble up the ladder of life. Land on a bad square and tumble down the chute. Game-maker Milton Bradley brought *Chutes and Ladders* to the U.S. in 1943, but it had originated in India 4,000 years earlier.

To educate children in Hindu philosophy, the ancient version used ladders to represent virtues and snakes to represent vices. Transported in 1892 to Victorian England as *Snakes and Ladders*, the game's ladders represented generosity, humility, and faith. Snakes were lust, anger, murder, and theft. The American version is tamer. Good deeds by which you ascend the ladder include mowing the lawn or saving a cat from a tree; drawing graffiti or eating too many cookies will plunge you into the abyss.

In a juridical version of *Chutes and Ladders*, the Frye case moved up and down Colorado's trial and appellate courts. The issue was Duane's confession. Lozow argued it was hearsay within hearsay. Hearsay is an out-of-court statement offered to prove the truth of what's said. Duane's confession was doubly complex because it was two statements: what he told his mother, Lolita; and what Lolita told his sister, Cherrie. It boiled down to how trustworthy Cherrie was.

On the eve of Duane's September 2008 trial, Judge Pratt wrestled with the confession. Neither he nor ADA Brackley had been present when Cherrie testified at the grand jury or at the pretrial hearing, and Brackley didn't offer to put Cherrie back on the stand. Was it because Brackley didn't want to deal with a feisty octogenarian who confused some of her dates, or because he wanted to dump the case?

Regardless, Pratt now had to rule on Cherrie's credibility without seeing how she held up under cross. Unable to fathom why Duane would confess to his mother, or why she would tell her daughter, Pratt threw out the confession.

Now Brackley faced a stark decision. Go to trial without the confession, or petition the Colorado Supreme Court to reverse Pratt? The petition was a long shot, but Brackley claimed the confession was so important he couldn't go to trial without it. He argued that neither Lolita nor Cherrie had a motive to lie, Cherrie's trustworthiness had already been tested in court, and Pratt should have focused on whether there was any reason for a mother to falsely accuse her son.

The petition was denied. Instead of going to trial without the confession, Brackley dismissed the case in order to file an appeal. Thus began a chutes-and-ladders trip through the higher courts. But whatever those courts decided, the DA's decision ended the case.

Before Duane could be retried, a grand jury would have to indict him a third time. Given his and other witnesses' ages, years of appeals promised a death knell to a new trial regardless of the appellate outcome. Worse, Brackley had tied any future DA's hands forever. In 1973, Duane had been indicted without a confession and might well have been convicted if not for Jim Blake and the ginned-up fingerprints. Now Brackley had handed Lozow the argument that the DA himself admitted there was no case without Duane's confession.

For four years, the Frye case limped through the appellate courts. Each day brought Duane a step closer to evading justice for good. And for those to whom Betty's death mattered, time finally did run out. While appeals were pending, both Dick Brickell and Betty's sister Agnes, surrogate mother to her seven younger sisters and rock of the Orten clan, died. Cherrie suffered a massive heart attack and was moved to a nursing home.

By the time the case reached the Colorado Court of Appeals, Brackley had left the Arapahoe County DA's Office. In 2010, the appellate court dismissed the case for lack of jurisdiction. The DA petitioned the Colorado Supreme Court for certiorari. In 2011, that court remanded the case to the Court of Appeals to decide whether Pratt properly threw out the confession.

In March 2012, thirty-nine years after Betty was murdered, seven years after the cold case was reignited, and four years after it began lurching its way through the appellate courts, the case came to a halt with the indignity of an unpublished opinion.

Duane's prosecution was over. He would never stand trial for his wife's murder.

But justice works in funny ways.

61. Case Files

The field of forensic science has come a very long way since its recorded beginning in the 700s, when the Chinese used fingerprints to establish the identity of documents and clay sculptures....

In 1248, a book, *Hsi Duan Yu* (the *Washing Away of Wrongs*), published by the Chinese, described how to distinguish drowning from strangulation. It was the first recorded application of medical knowledge to the solution of a crime. In 1609, the first treatise on systematic document examination was published in France. Then in 1784, one of the first documented uses of physical matching saw an Englishman convicted of murder based on the torn edge of a wad of newspaper in a pistol that matched a piece remaining in his pocket.
—**New York State Police Crime Laboratory System |**
Forensic Science History

As forensic science has evolved, case files have too.

Just decades ago, a file might be a few typed or handwritten pages and a half-dozen photos of the victim at the scene and the morgue. Physical evidence was a gun, a bludgeon, or a knife. Blood found at a distance wasn't collected, just photographed. In 1973, Bob Sendle wrote few reports because his job was putting the pieces together, not pounding the pavement. Negative observations—noting that something you'd expect to find was missing, say a nine-iron from a golf bag—weren't reported. By comparison, today's case files are encyclopedias.

In September 2012, after wrangling with the DA for a year and filing a request under the Colorado Open Records Act, I got the Frye file: thousands of pages of investigatory and crime lab reports, raw unfiltered notes, timelines, witness statements, and transcripts. Dozens of crime scene photos. Hours of audiotapes. Two-thirds in, I had to stop. I didn't return to the file for five months.

In May 2012, DA Tomsic let me sift through her file after she removed her work product, confidential medical records, and grand jury transcripts not attached to defense pleadings.

Each turn of a page brought a painful surprise.

Phone numbers, achingly familiar. The karate studio's sign-in sheets the day of the murder—kids like us, whose kicks and punches I could still picture. Jim Blake's obsession with Duane's clothes; he'd asked every witness but his report said my description—the most damaging to Duane—was most accurate. Nineteen-year-old Doug leaving the grand jury room to consult lawyer Leonard Davies on every question asked. Jan's boyfriend in Sunshine Canyon, whom Betty hated and where Jan spent the night before the murder, had a phone and Betty had the number. Betty on the autopsy table with her scalp peeled back and furrows plowed into her skull. Black spatters on the table-saw and pools on the garage floor. But the audiotapes instantly erased the passage of forty years.

Jan's voice throaty and hesitant, her heartbreaking pauses and inability to complete a sentence when asked about Betty's murder, turning to desperation and then rage as she realized Duane was the person they were still after. Doug so guarded and robotic he was scarcely audible, his voice lifting only at the very end when he asked if his dad would be arrested and the cop confirmed Duane was the only suspect. Lynn's ex-boyfriend Don recalling the crime scene like yesterday and the precise date Lynn walked out on him twelve years later. For each of us, it was as if time had stopped.

But the one for whom time had truly stopped was curiously absent from the file. In life and death, there was no place for Betty. In 1973 and the cold case, guilt and rage were aimed not at her killer, but at whoever did this to *them*. In the name of family, Betty's family redefined her right out of the case.

62. How Should the Story End?

Justice: The constant and perpetual disposition to render every man his due.
—*Black's Law Dictionary, Revised Fourth Edition*

---

closure 7: an often comforting or satisfying sense of finality.
—*Merriam-Webster's Collegiate Dictionary, Eleventh Edition*

I would like those kids—at least one of them—to actually admit, Yeah, my dad did it. None of the kids ever said, "Why aren't you out there looking for the person who killed my mother?" Instead it was, "Why do you even care anymore?"
—**Marv Brandt | 2011**

The word closure is an insult to the families of victims.
—**Howard Morton | Founder of Families of Homicide Victims and Missing Persons 2019**

In May 2011, facing the likelihood that Duane would never be prosecuted, I met with cold case cops Isaacson and Brandt. I asked them what they'd like to see happen. Brandt was outraged that none of Betty's kids cared enough about their mother to stand up for her. Isaacson was bitter about the DA's office dumping the case for the second time; out of twenty senior prosecutors in the room when the decision was made, he said Ann Tomsic was the only one who stood up and said going to trial was the right thing to do. Tomsic thought the biggest mistake after she left the case was Ryan Brackley not putting Cherrie back on the stand in front of the new judge, Pratt.

Tomsic herself never understood Duane's children. If she could ask one witness one question with the promise of a true answer, she told me, it would be what did those kids know. One thing she finds fascinating about cold cases is their effect on survivors' lives. She mentioned a case where a young woman's roommate was found raped and strangled in the bedroom after a party at their apartment. Two weeks later, a male guest at the same party was murdered. Both cases remain unsolved. Decades later, the woman told Tomsic she'd spent her life trying to fly under the radar; she described her life as having been very small. Tomsic thinks people need to feel safe, or at least understand what happened. Without closure, there's no sense of personal security.

Since there was no formal justice for Betty, what did the cold case accomplish?

Howard Morton founded FOHVAMP (Families of Homocide Victims and Missing Persons) because his eldest son, Guy, had been murdered in Arizona in 1975. Guy's murder is still unsolved. In 2005, after Cherrie told Jean that Duane had confessed, Jean called Morton. Morton brought Duane's confession to Bruce Isaacson.

In February 2019, I contacted Morton through LinkedIn. He remembered Betty's murder and *Quiet Time*. The next day, we talked by phone. Morton wanted to know what had happened to the case. Wasn't Duane's wife sick? he asked. Several FOHVAMP cases involved men who dominated their wives to the extent of making them physically ill. Morton had never heard of the Right Man syndrome, but he was describing it.

Under Morton, FOHVAMP had a simple criterion for choosing its cases: Was the family interested in finding justice? Over the years, he ran into one or two that didn't want a case reopened. In those cases, he suspected the families had something to do with the crime. If not, why wouldn't you want to know?

He'd also been on my website and read my blog about Betty's case. I'd always felt responsible for her murder— that by entering her family, I'd lit a fuse. What right did I have to write about it?

But Morton understood why I wrote *Quiet Time* and my connection to Betty's case. Until we spoke, I hadn't realized how much that mattered. Morton validated my right to care.

Morton also told me what the families of cold case victims really want. Not closure—the very word is an insult because the wound never heals. Bringing a killer to justice? For most, that's an impossible dream.

They want something simpler and more profound: to know what happened and why.

63. Bookends

Ms. Kane,

I am Investigator Bruce Isaacson with the Arapahoe County Sheriff's Office. Currently I am assigned the case of the murder of Elizabeth "Betty" Frye. Would you please contact me as soon as possible so that we may talk.

Thank you in advance for your time.

—Bruce

Hi Stephanie,

I wanted to let you know that Herbert Duane Frye committed suicide in April, 2013. I haven't found out yet if he left a note regarding the murder of his former wife, Betty, but I am still trying to find out if he finally admitted it…. I am friends with Barbara Frye's children and grandchildren. We all know he did it and he has exhibited behavior over the last 15 years that supports that he could do such a thing.

—[A Family Friend of Barb]

For me, the cold case is bookended by two e-mails: the one I received from Bruce Isaacson in November 2005, and the one from Barb's family friend in June 2013.

After speaking on the phone with her and the Florida cop who responded to the scene, I pieced together Duane's final years and the events surrounding his suicide.

If Duane was the Right Man, Barb was the Right Wife. And if Duane was Svengali, transforming a dowdy school marm with heavy glasses into the physical ideal Betty represented, Barb was a willing subject. Jean noticed the changes when Barb showed up at the first pretrial hearing. Barb's family friend, who'd known her since 1994, was surprised to hear Barb wasn't always slim and blonde. As long as she'd known her, Barb, as Duane's wife, was a manicured and pedicured lady with expensive jewelry and coordinated outfits. But Barb was well-educated and ambitious. Did she know who she was marrying?

When Doug and I dined at their Denver-area condo in the early 1980s, Duane angrily lashed out at Barb for forgetting to marinate the shrimp. She cowered but stayed with him, if not to the metaphorical ends of the earth, then at least to the extremes of the western hemisphere. Their marriage took them from Colorado to California and back, to Florida and Colorado and Florida again.

When Duane was arrested in 2006, Barb didn't tell her kids; a month later, when they saw it on TV, she still said nothing. When the cold case cops came to her door, the Right Wife clapped her hands in delight and exclaimed, You finally found who did it! But Barb's makeover and the house on the golf course had come at a price.

Duane kept his Right Wife on a tight leash. In Florida, they had no friends. Duane controlled Barb's social contacts, allowing her to belong only to an approved group of women who periodically met. When the cold case cops interviewed him there, he positioned himself at the end of his dining room table so he could continuously watch Barb with the local cop.

Barb and Duane kept their families separate. At Christmas, he went to Kansas. When she visited her kids on holidays and for birthdays in California, even telling him she was buying the tickets was difficult.

Tensions boiled over at a family dinner in an Italian restaurant southwest of Denver. Barb was chattering away, and when she wouldn't shut up, Duane became angry. He put his hands around her throat and made as if to throttle her. Leave my mother alone, her eldest daughter screamed. If I ever hear you touched her again, I'll kill you! She walked out, and that was the last time Barb's daughter and Duane were in the same room. Why did Barb stay?

Jim Dean didn't care that his wife wasn't stylish, but Duane did. His attention flattered and excited her. Barb was the Right Wife, whose missing ingredients—Betty's glamour and physical perfection—Duane could supply. But Barb, too, had her own power. She completed Duane. She was his submissive, adoring reflection staring back at him. The one person who looked at him every day in the way he wanted the world to see him. The only woman he could still dominate, the only one on the face of the earth who applauded and truly believed in him. The surrogate for his murdered wrong wife. Without Barb, the perfect spouse he tried to create in the image of poor failed Betty, who was Duane really?

Shortly before Christmas 2012, Barb suffered a stroke. She of the clapping hands was placed in a rehab center, on a slow slide into dementia. Through illness, Betty had deserted Duane. You're the strong one, he'd told Jean. I should have married you. Now Barb abandoned him too. He was back to where he'd begun: a helpless child in a hostile universe.

In April 2013, Lynn was living with her father. One day when she left for work, she asked a neighbor to check in on him, and gave him the garage door opener. The next morning, the neighbor tried to call Duane. Receiving no answer, he entered the house through the garage. He found Duane in his glassed-in patio facing the golf course. He'd put a shotgun to his head and fired.

Duane could have left his motor running in the garage. He could have overdosed on prescription pills or driven to a deserted place and shot himself. Or hung in to care for his Right Wife, the one he said he loved. But he did it his way. This final horrific act was meant to be discovered by someone he knew and to leave an indelible mark. It said: *Look what you made me do.*

Duane left a suicide note. It referred to Barb's declining health but didn't mention his first wife.

It expressed no remorse.

64. Character Arc

arc 1: the apparent path described above and below the horizon by a celestial body (as the sun)
—Merriam-Webster's Collegiate Dictionary, Eleventh Edition

A character arc is the transformation or inner journey of a character over the course of a story.
—Wikipedia

There is no refuge from confession but suicide, and suicide is confession.
—Daniel Webster | Summation in the murder trial of John Francis Knapp 1830

The writer's holy grail is character arc. From Joseph Campbell's *The Hero with a Thousand Faces* to Chris Vogler's *The Writer's Journey*, to Robert McKee's *Story: Style, Structure, Substance, and the Principles of Screenwriting*, we're taught that unless the protagonist changes at the end, there's no story. In Colin Wilson's *A Criminal History of Mankind*, in the end the Right Man destroys himself.

In March 2011, when I phoned Cherrie at The Verandas, the assisted- care facility where she was living, the first thing she said was, Duane's still alive, isn't he? Her fear was unmistakable. After Duane committed suicide, I called Cherrie's ex-husband Hank, who asked me not to tell her. Cherrie outlived her brother by more than six months, but never knew Duane was dead. Frightened, embittered, and convinced that coming forward with Duane's confession was the worst mistake of her life, she died in a nursing home on Thanksgiving Day 2013.

Duane's suicide bookended Betty's murder. The parallels are stark: violent death by massive intentional trauma to the head, at home where the body would be found by a family member. Suicide by shotgun blast to the head is a uniquely brutal and horrific act that leaves an indelible mark on survivors. Doing it at home— where Lynn lived with him—ensured someone he knew would not only find him but would also be shocked. Duane's act of guilt, violence, and rage ended his family's arc.

Coda

65. Retribution

The dice of God are always loaded.... Every secret is told, every crime is punished, every virtue rewarded, every wrong redressed, in silence and certainty....[Fear is] a carrion crow, and though you see not well what he hovers for, there is death somewhere... Inasmuch as he carries the malignity and the lie with him, he so far deceases from nature... [T]his deadly deduction makes square his eternal account.
—**Ralph Waldo Emerson** | *Compensation*

In spite of Virtue and the Muse, Nemesis will have her dues.
—**Ralph Waldo Emerson** | *Nemesis*

The goddess of retribution is Nemesis. Her name comes from the Greek word *némein*, "to give what is due." Hunting down the guilty and standing beside the judges of the dead, Nemesis lets no crime go unpunished. She lured Narcissus to the woodland pool, where he fell in love with his own reflection and wasted away because he couldn't possess it. Her main target is Hubris.

Aristotle defined Hubris as shaming a victim for personal gratification. *Against Meidias*, a fourth century

B.C. oration by the Greek statesman Demosthenes, was occasioned by Demosthenes's old enemy, the wealthy Meidias, publicly slapping him in the face. In *Against Conon*, Demosthenes pled the cause of Ariston, a young Athenian, after Conon and his sons emptied their chamber pots and urinated on Ariston's slaves. When Ariston rebuked Conon, Conon stripped Ariston naked, trampled him into a thick puddle of mud, and beat him so viciously he vomited blood.

Hubris means arrogance before the gods, and throughout literature Nemesis has followed in winged pursuit. With predictable results, Man defies God in Milton's *Paradise Lost*, Marlowe's *Doctor Faustus,* and Mary Shelley's *Frankenstein.*

The two volumes of Ian Kershaw's biography of Adolph Hitler are called *Hubris*, chronicling Hitler's early life and rise to power, and *Nemesis*, his fall and suicide. But to nineteenth century American essayist and poet Ralph Waldo Emerson, *Nemesis* was more elemental.

She squared the accounts.

In Emerson's 1841 essay *Compensation*, he writes that crime and punishment grow from a single stem. Each act has two inseparable qualities: its nature (cause) and the circumstances that follow (effect). Just as the fruit exists in the seed, the end pre-exists the means. The fact that the law may fail, and retribution be spread over many years, does not mean justice is postponed. Offenses are speedily punished by fear—that carrion crow. Did it hover over Duane?

Justice is restored when the malignancy a killer carries within deceases him from nature. That day in April 2013, with the morning paper still on his kitchen counter, Duane Frye put a shotgun to his head and squared his eternal account.

66. Guilt

complicity/1: association or participation in or as if in a wrongful act
—Merriam-Webster's Collegiate Dictionary, Eleventh Edition

This is the first of punishments, that no guilty man is acquitted if judged by himself.
—Juvenal

Doug and I didn't talk about Betty's murder.

In 1973, Duane controlled what we were told. The cops never questioned me, and as a grand jury witness, Doug was warned not to talk. At the bail hearing, Duane's lawyers parked us and his sisters in the front row and marched us out of the courtroom when the DA produced the crime scene photos. Before Lynn moved East later that summer and Greg was sent to the opposite coast, there was no discussion about what had happened. When I tried to talk to Mom, she dismissed me. I worried that Doug would never smile or laugh again.

Duane's trial was set to start the Monday after

Thanksgiving. That weekend, when he phoned to tell us the charges had been dropped, we were on a delayed three-day honeymoon in Winter Park, Colorado. Back in Boulder, we went to a shop on Pearl Street looking for a card to send him. We spotted the perfect one: a dog jumping a fence, captioned *Free at last!* We left empty-handed.

Duane and Barb married and moved with Greg to California. The rest of Doug's family scattered. The karate studio we had opened became a stepping-stone to law and med school. We bought a house in a development northeast of Boulder, then moved into town. The past was in the rearview mirror, until that trip to New York, when Doug and Lynn finally did talk.

Doug cleared out before I knew he was gone. He took his childhood photos, leaving a half-empty wedding album and no trace of a shared past—just memories of fleeting joy, a marriage that had died with his mother, and my conviction that the abortion and our wedding were to blame. If we didn't kill Betty, we certainly pushed her over the edge.

On the stand in 2005, Duane's lawyers pummeled me about my so-called duty to come forward. If what I was saying now was true, why didn't I go to the cops in 1973? The judge cut off this line of questioning—there is no such duty.

But the question hit a truer mark. What was I really protecting back then? My rocky place in Doug's family, the need for our marriage to succeed, the fantasy that closing my eyes could make a murder go away? Guilty as charged.

But one thing haunts me still.

If I could do it over, would I?

67. Grief

I think that's the hardest part, in some ways, having that sequence take place. That the first event gets… sort of buried almost, in the energy and intent going on with the second event which is more eminent and much more right here, right now… I've always felt that none of my family actually grieved well for my mother, because days later, my father was arrested, and then the attention went right there.
—**Jan Frye | 2006**

Early, major loss can derail a life narrative and shatter a child's sense of safety and assumptions about a future.
—**Hope Edelman |** *I Can't Say 'My Mother' Without Crying*

And then you kind of re-form yourself in this quiet, grieving world that was created in the house.
—**Stephen Colbert | 2019**

Skin is the body's largest organ. Far bigger than the brain, it excretes toxins, and it filters what we allow in. It's the envelope enclosing our shape, defining where we end and the outer world begins.

It is also a potent metaphor. Thin-skinned people are overly sensitive. Skin in the game means personal risk. To save your own skin is to survive at any cost. As an old law professor of mine once said, Every life has a shape, and people will fight like hell to preserve it.

As a teenager, Hope Edelman lost her mother to breast cancer. In a 2019 *New York Times* op-ed, she said grief has no quick or easy fix.

CNN has interviewed Anderson Cooper, whose father died of a heart attack when he was 10, and Stephen Colbert, who'd lost his father and two brothers in a plane crash at the same age. Colbert has spoken of re-forming himself in grief. Cooper said his father's death changed his life's trajectory, that he was a different person than he felt he was meant to be.

Edelman's 2019 op-ed struck a chord. Sixty or seventy years after a parent died, readers wrote in to say they continued to mourn.

But grief needs space.

To preserve a life's shape, we filter the unbearable out or reduce it to a sequence. A mother's murder becomes an event, a father's arrest another. One displaces the other; fighting like hell sucks the oxygen from the room and puts you back in charge.

But if you deny how your mom died or who was responsible, can you grieve for her? And if grief is the ticket to acceptance, a quiet space to re-form, how do you find your new place in the world without it?

68. Truth vs. Honesty

truth/3a: the property (as of a statement) of being in accord with fact or reality
—Merriam-Webster's Collegiate Dictionary, Eleventh Edition

---

honesty/2a: fairness and straightforwardness of conduct; b: adherence to the facts
—Merriam-Webster's Collegiate Dictionary, Eleventh Edition

Truthiness refers to the quality of seeming to be true but not necessarily or actually true according to known facts.
—Merriam-Webster's 2006 Word of the Year

[In a post-truth world, our] allegiance as nonfiction writers is not so much to truth as it is to honesty. Because truth can be spoken into a void, while honesty implies an audience, a reader, real people to whom you commit to tell your story as accurately and truthfully as you can so that they can then differentiate for themselves the facts from the lies, the truth from the fiction.
*—**Sarah Viren** | The Accusation*

Sarah Viren is a creative-nonfiction writing teacher. In 2019, she and her wife, a linguistics professor, were falsely accused of sexual harassment by an unnamed person posing as a graduate student.

The accuser, who stalked Viren on social media and Reddit, was ultimately unmasked as a male academic competing against her for a coveted teaching post— but not until both women's careers had been derailed and they'd filed a lawsuit against him.

The university's Kafkaesque investigation into the accusation is almost as harrowing as the lies the accuser spun. But most pernicious of all were the self-doubts those lies spawned in Viren.

True Crime Redux is my best effort to come to grips with Betty's death based on facts. In 1973, did I know Duane killed her? No. But I never doubted what I'd witnessed: The dynamics at their dinner table. Betty telling me Duane had blown up at a woman from the phone company. What he was wearing the day of the murder. The injury to his forehead. Duane abruptly rising from the daybed in our apartment and announcing he had to leave.

Impressions are interpretations of facts. I interpreted Duane's dinner table behavior as an assertion of control over his family that went beyond anti-Semitic rants and a curt demand to be passed the peas. I understood what Betty told me about the phone company incident to mean she was more worried about Duane than she was about herself. The day of the murder, Duane's clothing, demeanor, and behavior were out of sync, not just with the weather, but with any version of him I'd encountered before.

For honesty and truth to mean anything, observable phenomena can't just be up for grabs. Every writer brings his or her own perceptions to their work, but nonfiction should at least attempt to accord with reality and adhere to facts. Truthiness—that "as if" netherworld where fever dreams are elevated to half-truths—belongs elsewhere.

69. Mercy

mercy/1 Forbearance and compassion shown to a
powerless person, esp. an offender, or to one with no
claim to receive kindness; kind and compassionate
treatment in a case where severity is merited or
expected.
—*The New Shorter Oxford English Dictionary*

For Mercy has a human heart, Pity a human face,
And Love, the human form divine,
And Peace, the human dress.
—**William Blake |** *The Divine Image*

For justice, the Greeks looked to the gods.

The first woman, Pandora, was given a jar as a wedding
gift. The jar contained the evils of the earth, along with
the good: Trust, Hope, the Graces, and Restraint.
Pandora was warned not to open the jar. Unable to
resist, she did, unleashing most of the virtues and all of
the evils on the world. Freed, the evils roamed the earth,
and Trust, the Graces, and Restraint fled back to
Olympus. When Pandora slammed down the lid,
humankind was left only with Hope.

When a murderer walks, the opposite occurs. Truth is cast to the winds, and the jar becomes a vacuum. In rush hatred, destruction, madness, cruelty—lies. Bottled up, they ferment and metastasize. Without hope, those trapped inside can't escape. All are punished. Even the guilty.

But mercy has a human heart.

Mercy isn't lofty or grandiloquent, but tender and small. You can ask for it but not demand it. You can hope for it, but you can't expect it because you have no right to it. Because it's undeserved, it's solely within the grantor's discretion. It's not a transaction; it is a gift.

Mercy isn't a pardon. A pardon is restorative; by returning you to the person who committed no wrong, it erases the act.

Mercy recognizes and accepts the wrong. It recognizes your human worth despite—and because of—your failings.

Retribution can be spread over years. Mercy just takes one phone call.

70. Fade out

fade out: a filmmaking and broadcasting technique whereby an image is made to disappear gradually or the sound volume is gradually decreased to zero.
—dictionary.com

On Easter Sunday 2014, I was at my computer when Jean Brickell called. She and John chatted, then he gave me the phone.

Jean wished me a happy Easter, and I asked how she was. My usual horrible aches and pains, she said with her trilling laugh; at 88, she was having people over later for crepes and Easter eggs.

The reason for her call? She was upset about an abortion bill that would legalize over-the-counter day-after pills without parental consent. The Archbishop had read a fabulous letter in church that morning, Jean said, and as Catholics we're all praying this horrible thing won't pass. She wanted John and me to contact our state legislators.

Did she forget the original sin committed by the Jewish girl from Brooklyn? Maybe it no longer mattered.

Our conversation roamed. Her sister Thelma was going

blind, and the ophthalmologist was trying to convince her to replace her eye with an artificial one because the drops were painful.

I'd just lost my brother, and Jean wanted his name so she could pray for him. It was comforting to talk to her about losing a sibling; not everything came straight back to Betty.

But Jean was preoccupied with Greg, whom she was convinced held the key. None of the Frye kids had been in touch with their aunts. I'd always said I planned to write about the case, and before we hung up, I told her that again. God love you, she said, and thank you for not forgetting.

The last time I heard from Jean was in 2018, when we exchanged Christmas cards. On hers were Mary, Jesus, and the Three Maji. I have no news from the Fryes, she wrote. Stay well and happy. God Bless! She signed it Mom Jean Brickell.

My 2019 card went unanswered. I found her obit on the web.

Rest in peace, Jean.

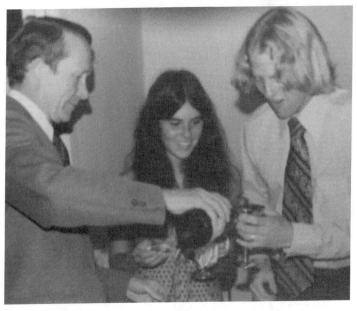

From Betty and me, Duane said as he toasted us with glasses he'd thrown in the trash moments after beating his wife to death. (p. 33)

About the Author

Stephanie Kane is a lawyer and award-winning author of seven crime novels. After graduating from law school, she was a corporate partner at a top Denver law firm before becoming a criminal defense attorney. She has lectured on money laundering and white-collar crime in Eastern Europe, and given workshops throughout the country on writing technique.

Her crime novels have won a Colorado Book Award for Mystery and two Colorado Authors League Awards for Genre Fiction. She belongs to the Mystery Writers of America, Rocky Mountain Fiction Writers, and the Colorado Authors League.

She lives in Denver with her husband and two black cats.